Vanished!

explorers *forever* **lost**

Vanished!

explorers *forever* lost

Evan Balkan

MENASHA RIDGE PRESS
Birmingham, Alabama

Copyright © 2008 by Evan Balkan
All rights reserved
Published by Menasha Ridge Press
Printed in the United States of America
Distributed by Publishers Group West
First edition, first printing

Library of Congress Cataloging-in-Publication Data

Balkan, Evan, 1972–
    Vanished!: explorers forever lost/by Evan Balkan. —1st ed.
       p. cm.
    ISBN-13: 978-0-89732-983-5
    ISBN-10: 0-89732-983-X
       1. Explorers—United States—Biography. 2. Explorers—England—
    Biography. I. Title.
    G200.B25 2007
    910.92'273—dc22
                        2007031159

Text and cover design by Travis Bryant
Cover photograph by Greg Balfour Evans/Alamy
Author photograph (page vii) by Erik Balkan
Percy Fawcett photo (page 21) courtesy of the Library of Congress
Everett Ruess photo (page 53) courtesy of the University of Utah
Indexing by Galen Schroeder

Menasha Ridge Press
P.O. Box 43673
Birmingham, Alabama 35243
www.menasharidge.com

Table of
Contents

For Erik. Here's to the great trips—and always returning home.

About the Author

Evan Balkan teaches writing at the Community College of Baltimore County. His fiction and nonfiction, mostly in the areas of travel and outdoor recreation, have been published throughout the United States as well as in Canada, England, and Australia. A graduate of Towson, George Mason, and Johns Hopkins universities, he is also the author of *60 Hikes within 60 Miles: Baltimore* (Menasha Ridge Press). He lives in Lutherville, Maryland, with his wife, Shelly, and daughters, Amelia and Molly.

[A] voice, as bad as Conscience, rang interminable changes
On one everlasting Whisper day and night repeated—so:
"Something hidden. Go and find it. Go and look behind the Ranges—
Something lost behind the Ranges. Lost and waiting for you. Go!"

—Rudyard Kipling, "The Explorer"

1. Ambrose Bierce (1914)

2. Percy Fawcett (1925)

3. Glen and Bessie Hyde (1928)

4. Everett Ruess (1934)

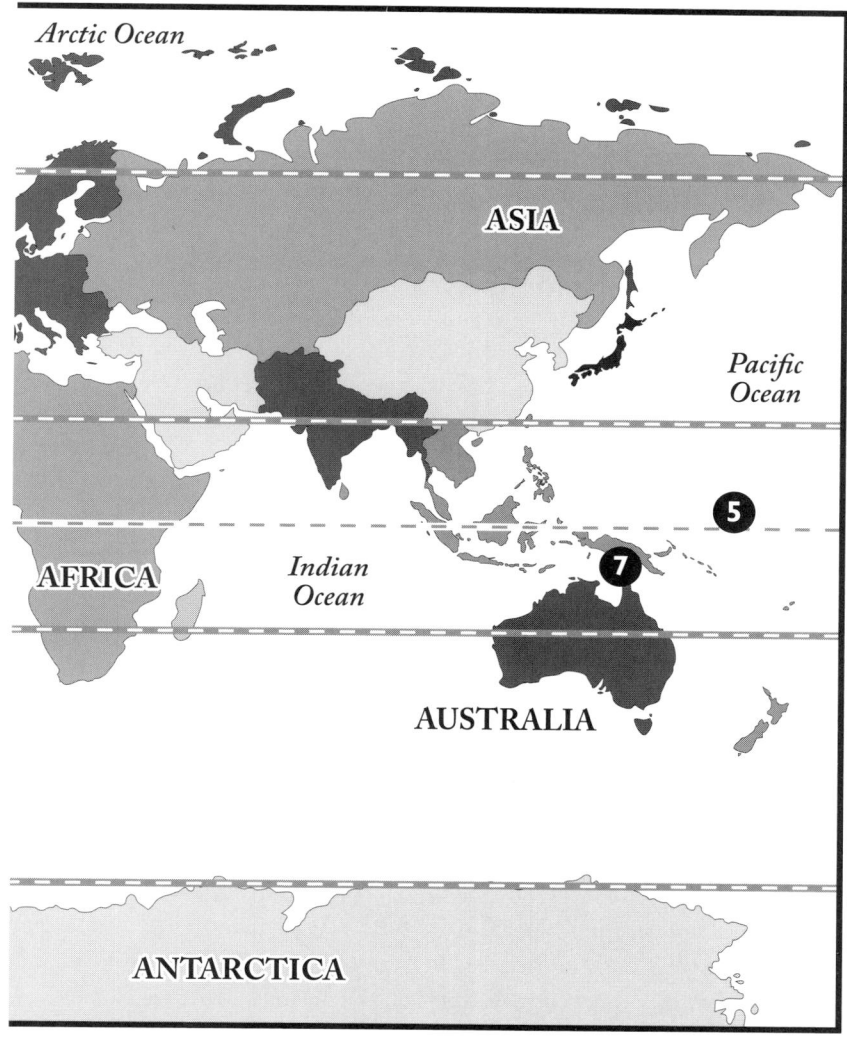

⑤ Amelia Earhart (1937)

⑥ Antoine de Saint-Exupéry (1944)

⑦ Michael Rockefeller (1961)

⑧ Johnny Waterman (1981)

Preface

I had just graduated from college, and the time was ripe for setting off—so I embarked on a circle trek around Western Europe. I left in the summer and didn't return home until November. It was only the second time I had left the country.

During that trip, I fell in with some interesting characters. There was an Aussie named Paul who spent a solid fifteen to twenty minutes each morning ritualistically clearing his throat, upper chest, and sinuses. It created a repellent din, a churning of internal mechanisms designed, best I could tell, to awaken the recently dead.

In Galway, Ireland, Paul's ceremony was preceded several times during the night by the spectacle of a German somnambulist who screamed maniacally before settling into a paroxysm of giggles. In the predawn darkness, I managed to nod off for an hour before being awakened by a massive, filthy foot from the upper bunk feeling its way for the floor and finding my face instead. It was all terribly annoying at the time, but these bits became memories as precious to me as those of first descending into London's tube, climbing the Eiffel Tower, visiting the Prado in Madrid, or trekking along the pass from Italy through northwest Slovenia to Austria. All of it was, at the time, my "grand adventure," an experience that required me to step out of my comfort zone and gleefully imbibe whatever this foreign world promised me—good or bad. In the end, it was all good.

There would be many subsequent trips inside and outside the United States, these with the benefit of more savvy packing on my part. Instead of lugging forty pounds through a dozen countries, I would lighten my load by jettisoning such superfluous items as Q-tips and realizing that three T-shirts was plenty: wear each one two or three times, and manage to wash them once or twice along the way. Trips these days are tailored to the company—whether I'm traveling with my wife, with the kids, with my brother, or with friends, the scenery and the expectations change accordingly. But in each case—in every single one—there is a common denominator: each time I leave my home and purposefully immerse myself in something foreign—even if the changes are as subtle as, say, the slight cultural shift involved in leaving my home in Baltimore and visiting the Carolinas—I'm forced to confront something out of my immediate comfort zone, and I'm forced to change what would otherwise be the easy routine of home.

Of course, routine is underrated; the vast majority of the world's population strives to reach something resembling the comfortable routine that I've come to enjoy: wake early, get the kids ready for day care, spend an hour or two at home writing or reading, and trace the familiar route to my work at the college. At night, my wife, kids, and I meet at the dinner table, reveling in the closeness we're lucky to share.

Sometimes I stand back and look at it all, and as sleep-deprived and kid-crazied as I get at times, I thank whatever lucky stars aligned to give me the scene I have before me. Family, friends, work, creative pursuits—it's all there just as I want it.

But if I'm honest—and you'll forgive me here for a bit of therapeutic admission—I have to acknowledge The Itch. The Itch is something every person stricken with wanderlust knows about. It's the thing that makes you wake at night, go grab the oversize atlas off the shelf, and run your finger along the hippie trail from Varanasi to Kabul. You look at those lines on the page, the great blank spaces, the megalopolises represented by stars and bolded script, and you wonder what they look like in person. You start to plan, to figure out a way to get to those places. At once, there in a chilly room bumping up against three in the morning, you decide that seeing Angkor Wat is suddenly the most important thing in the world. And you look on those who would think you're crazy for doing so with something like pity—what do they know anyway?

Actually, I don't feel pity for such people. Instead, in a way I envy them. After all, I'm quite certain that they don't lie awake at night as I have, feeling somehow incomplete because they've never trekked to the top of Mount Roraima, the meeting point of Venezuela, Brazil, and Guyana. They haven't sleepwalked through days until the desire, the need to make it to that spot, slowly melts away until seeing the destination is something that I can live without, only to have it replaced by the need to get to someplace else.

My brother and I sometimes engage in little travel competitions—who has been to more countries (me), oceans (him), seas (me), continents (him), etc. But these are just games, and we both know it. (Besides, when we get to a place together, such as Peru, the fact that we add to our lists simultaneously is more thrilling than anything else.) After all, one of the most memorable places I've ever been wasn't abroad; it was in the desert Southwest of this country. What matters is not to add to the checklist, but to have a life transformed by a place that forces you to question everything you know. I once met a guy from

Burkina Faso who asked me if in the area where I grew up, there was "rock" all over the ground. I finally figured out that he was talking about sidewalks. Imagine that: pouring concrete over the perfectly fine ground for no other reason than to protect my shoes from getting dirty. Indeed, I walk out my door, get in the car, drive, park, and walk into a building at work, never once touching the earth. Whether this is an unnecessary and gross extravagance or a simple luxury I should be grateful for, I'm not sure. But I do know that after that conversation with the fellow from Burkina Faso, I never had a walk that wasn't colored by his very simple question that was, in its way, one of the most complex things I've ever pondered.

That's a healthy exercise, in every way. It's why I'm rarely happier than when I'm smacked in the head by some exquisite show of nature or human culture that is far from the front door I open every morning. It needs to be said that I love nothing more than being behind that door, with the people I love.

But to get back out, to see the world . . . that remains essential.

This book highlights nine people infected with The Itch. You've no doubt heard of some of them; perhaps others will be new to you. Each of their stories is unique, but they all share the same common denominator I wrote of above. Each of these people couldn't be contented with the comfortable life in front of him or her. They had to walk out that door and put themselves in places that challenged them physically and emotionally. For that, they should be admired and celebrated. However, many readers will see selfish foolishness in their actions, for they left behind grieving friends, spouses, parents, children. Some critics could argue that because of their willingness to go anyway, these people are to be not admired, but reviled. Of course, this revulsion at their selfishness is inevitably mixed with approbation for their feats. Concerning the adventurer, Antoine de Saint-Exupéry wrote, "There is a tendency to class such men with toreadors and gamblers. People extol their contempt for death. But I would not give a fig for anybody's contempt for death. If its roots are not sunk deep in an acceptance of responsibility, this contempt for death is the sign either of an impoverished soul or of youthful extravagance."

True enough, but in the end, something compelled these people to push themselves to their limits, and what a boring world we would live in indeed if such people didn't walk among us. They deserve our veneration and gratitude for the advancement of knowledge each gave us, even if that knowledge was limited to understanding how to engage in like feats without succumbing.

Each of these stories is also a cautionary tale. For in every one of these cases, these people never came back home. They engaged in that one last great voyage that left them somewhere out there, their respective fates to be pondered by generations hence. In so doing, they left great mysteries worthy of the extraordinary nature of their undertakings. In doing everything from testing the limits of aviation to climbing uncharted mountains, from venturing into desolate landscapes to plunging into impenetrable jungles in search of lost cities, from seeking "primitive" cultures to testing the mighty forces of one of the world's great natural wonders, from seeking one last great adventure to seeking alternatives to accepted routes and ways of thinking, the men and women in this book were large in scope and vision, and each left an outsize stamp on those who knew and loved them. They each constitute a fantastic story. But it must be remembered that these were real human beings, and their absences no doubt caused many to grieve. Saint-Exupéry understood this as well. He knew that behind the grand story, the one we are sometimes compelled to turn away from, there are at heart just simple people—and in the end we are all just simple people. "Every week," he wrote in 1939, "men sit comfortably at the cinema and look on at the bombardment of some Shanghai or other, some Guernica, and marvel without a trace of horror at the long fringes of ash and soot that twist their slow way into the sky from those man-made volcanoes. Yet we all know that together with the grain in the granaries, with the heritage of generations of men, with the treasures of families, it is the burning flesh of children and their elders that, dissipated in smoke, is slowly fertilizing those black cumuli.

The physical drama itself cannot touch us until someone points out its spiritual sense. In writing this book, I felt that I got to know these people, the "spiritual sense" within the "physical drama." And it was a privilege living with them as I did the research for this book.

In so doing, it was impossible not to envision myself in their final moments—or their assumed final moments, anyway. All of them must have felt, if only for a fleeting moment, the sickening sensation of abandonment.

An infant who has only his physical needs met will soon succumb to a host of infirmities. The emotional and psychological connection to other humans is essential for development. As we age, this abates somewhat, but never really leaves us. Even the most stoic existentialist has to feel a flash of terror at the notion of dying so unutterably alone. For even if one has physical company, the very final moments are one's alone—to contemplate, to question (perhaps regret), finally to accept.

We've all desired solitude every now and again. Some of us can return to the ones we love only after first experiencing the tests of seclusion; we purposefully set out into the wilderness and come back changed. We come to realize that we and we alone are the authors of our fate. Should we get stuck or lost, when all hope appears gone and we've given up, we look to the sky and plead for help. The response is a distant twinkling of star, and we get up and muddle through. We call on the reserves we scarcely knew we possessed. We conjure up primal instincts we assumed had long ago been dashed. We make it somehow, and we return to our comfortable world better able to navigate all aspects of this life because we know now that, in the end, everything is up to ourselves.

And then, sometimes, there is no coming back. There are times when even the most prepared finally falls to ill luck, circumstance, or the unarguable fact that a solitary human is really no match for the forces of nature.

It's not so terribly easy to go missing these days. To get lost, yes. To succumb, sure. But at some point, the remains will be found. Indeed, it's a lamentable fact for many outdoor enthusiasts that they don't get to have "isolated" spots to themselves. There's a story I like to tell about something that happened a few years ago while I was in the American Southwest.

I was in a rental car, and I ditched the pavement somewhere in the Painted Desert in northern Arizona, turning onto a dirt track that ran through the Navajo Indian Reservation. But when the dirt track itself appeared no longer distinguishable from the parched desert floor, I finally began to feel apart—experiencing that horrible, but wonderful, realization that I could die out there if my car broke down. Only when I felt certain that this was the case did I stop my car to breathe in the scene before me.

The horizon appeared endless, a stretch of sky rent in two by thin wisps of cloud, which separated evenly to reveal a bluer shade of blue than I had ever thought possible. I was alone—"home," but nowhere near home. I was greatly disappointed then when I turned around and saw a faint cloud of dust, accompanied by the low rumble of an engine. Soon, a Toyota Land Cruiser pulled up. The Land Cruiser stopped, and an older man stepped from the car.

"Thought you had it all to yourself?" the man asked, with an accent I couldn't quite place. "You from around here?" he continued.

"No. I live on the East Coast," I told him. "Two thousand miles away. Closer than your home, I suspect," I said, trying to be folksy.

"Just a bit. I'm from Wellington, New Zealand. You've been?"

"No. I'd love to though. Closest I came was sharing a room in a hostel in London with a guy from Wellington . . . You wouldn't happen to know a fellow named Lance G____?" I asked, half-joking. "He was my London hostel-mate about eight years ago."

It's difficult to avoid the cliché, but there is no way around it: the man almost fell over from shock. Lance was his son.

Of course, coincidences can happen anywhere, but our little game of connect-the-dots spanned three continents, almost a decade of time, and more than twenty thousand miles.

Had my car broken down out there, had I wandered the desert in search of habitation, either the fellow from Wellington, or some Navajo on horseback or in a pickup, or just some adventurer like me would have come across my body. Calls would have been made, some tears would have been shed, I like to think, and I would have ended up the subject of a memorial service and proper burial.

It used to be different. When the world was a more or less uncharted place, people set out to map the corners of the earth, mostly spurred on by economic interests. Nevertheless, adventure for adventure's sake was then, and still is, a great motivator in itself. But back when the planet had vast unmapped spots, people went missing as a matter of course. The entire Roanoke settlement of more than one hundred colonists disappeared sometime around 1590, the word *Croatan* carved into a post the only remnant of the community. In the first year of that same century, the Portuguese explorer Gaspar Corte-Real disappeared while on an expedition to discover the Northwest Passage from Europe to Asia. Gaspar Corte-Real is credited with discovering Greenland in 1500, and on his subsequent journey he disappeared. His brother Miguel went searching for him in 1502. He also disappeared.

With the hindsight of five centuries, it's easy to dismiss people such as the Corte-Reals as a foolhardy bunch for intentionally setting off into the unknown wilds in search of elusive fame and fortune, especially when the fortune a successful expedition would bring often landed in the hands not of the explorers but of the already-wealthy sponsors.

But such a dismissal fails to take into account that the treasures gained along the route outweigh monetary riches, make a mockery of posterity, and render the backward-looking observers of later millennia foolish for their failure to understand. Yes, the Northwest Passage claimed two brothers (and might have claimed a third, Vasco Anes, had not the Portuguese king refused to subsequently send him). But what these men must have seen during their journeys! What amazing sights must narwhals, polar bears, and Asiatic-looking men living in ice houses have been to these men from a temperate land not far from the Tropic of Cancer.

The memories of such places and such sights would no doubt have been enough to sustain them through any lonely night at sea (or back home on safe land), any pounding Atlantic storm, or any quickened pulse or faint rumble of misgiving. It's something of a theme we can see in all of the explorers in this book. They go to places that severely test them, and while they may express gratitude at having gotten back from such places, it isn't long before they decide they must return. The pull of the wild is a force beyond the comprehension of anyone who hasn't felt it. The British explorer Percy Harrison Fawcett, chronicled in this book in Chapter Two, after having survived some rather hellish moments in the jungles of Bolivia, wrote of being home at last in safe, cozy, and familiar England: "I spent Christmas at home. The well-behaved English winter passed swiftly and evenly, as though South America had never been. Yet deep inside me a tiny voice was calling. At first scarcely audible, it persisted until I could no longer ignore it. It was the voice of the wild places, and I knew that it was now part of me for ever."

And in the case of the Corte-Real brothers, they probably had little choice in returning anyway. They were the sons of another explorer, João Vaz Corte-Real, who, it is believed, landed in North America a full twenty years before Columbus's celebrated voyage. The sons then had a genetic disposition toward exploration; no doubt listening wide-eyed to their father's tales assured that a sedentary life would be impossible. Any young child today who sits in front of an atlas, under the covers with a flashlight while unsuspecting parents watch TV in another room, knows the feeling. He draws his finger over maps, wondering—almost bursting at the thought of it—what these little lines of paper actually look like in their real positions on this wild and wondrous planet. The exotic names—Cappadocia, Oaxaca, Ulaanbaatar—they practically scream for discovery. And as we know, even a city with a million inhabitants is a place waiting to be discovered if we've never been there before. The secrets and solicitudes, the thrills and fears—they are so very different though as equally there for the taking in a megalopolis such as São Paulo as in the distant jungles of Borneo.

In the words of naturalist and explorer Roy Chapman Andrews, "Always there has been an adventure just around the corner—and the world is still full of corners."

—Evan Balkan

Foreword

By Richard Bangs

If but a safe voyage is sought, the boat should never leave the harbor.

Yet if the ambition is discovery, or telluric wisdom, or the evolution of consciousness, or even the crasser quests of religious, political, or economic booty, then sails must billow, waves must be crested, and risks assumed. Without risk there can be no reward; but with it comes the proposition that one might not come back.

In the Age of Exploration, adventurers were most often severely financed souls willing to trade limb and life in search of plum for their backers. This was closer to war than romance in that participants often lived in mortifying dread; supped on hard biscuits, sawdust, and rats; and slept lonely on hard surfaces in hopes of returning to a better life, a bit richer, perhaps with a promotion and some fame. More often than not, these adventures were distinguished by their accidents, either in geographic discovery, disappearance, or loss of life; they were, in essence, well-planned trips gone wrong. Leif Ericsson was blown off course during a voyage from Norway to Greenland about 1000 AD, and knocked into North America. Nearly five centuries later, Columbus imagined he had arrived in the Indies, when he was in fact half a world away in the Caribbean.

Almost thirty years later, Ferdinand Magellan was looking for a western trade route to the Spice Islands when he came to a sticky end in a local skirmish in the Philippines; likewise, Ponce de León, Étienne Brûlé, Captain Cook, John Gilbert, and Jedediah Smith were killed by indigenes during their explorations. Vitus Bering died of exposure navigating the northern sea that would bear his surname, Henry Hudson disappeared in his namesake bay after he was put adrift in a small boat by a mutinous crew, and Scottish doctor Mungo Park vanished while navigating the Niger River. John Franklin lost his entire expedition, two ships and 129 men, when he became icebound trying to negotiate the Northwest Passage. And while Henry Morton Stanley survived his 999-day journey across the malarial midriff of the Dark Continent, half of his 359 men did not. Robert Falcon Scott may have been a last of breed, sacrificing himself and his party to an Antarctic storm for the sake of science (he dragged rocks and specimens across the continent to within eleven miles of a resupply depot) and of British boasting rights to be the first to the South Pole (Norwegian Roald Amundsen beat him by five weeks).

The point is, these adventures were decidedly dangerous, and, like men enlisting to go to battle, those who volunteered had the grim expectation they might not return. These were souls willing to go where only dragons marked the map, and to tender lives for queen, country or God, or the trading company. If there was any personal gratification or growth that came from the exercise, it was tangential . . . the central goal was to survive, and come home with bounty, be it new colonies, converted souls, slaves, spices or knowledge.

The next historiographical trend in exploration had its archetype in Richard Burton, who, though commissioned by the English East India Company and later the Royal Geographical Society, really set about exploring to satisfy his own insatiable curiosity about foreign life, languages, and exotic sex. He was a new-fashioned adventurer, who sought out perfectly unnecessary hazards in the name of inquisitiveness and pursued the unknown not for empire or some larger good, but for his own love of discovery.

Ernest Shackleton was another early executant of this sensibility. For his ill-conceived plan to cross the Antarctic he had major sponsors, and he promoted his "imperial" expedition as scientific, though he had no interest in science, even scorned it. The real reasons for the extreme endeavor were personal: he loved a good adventure; loved the romantic notion of searching for fortune; and loved to sing, jig, and joke with his mates in the field. Everything else was an excuse.

Others came to personify this type of adventure in a more direct way, such as New Zealand beekeeper Ed Hillary, who clearly had a vast enthusiasm for climbing and was able to parlay it to membership on a high-profile British Himalayan expedition, and Wilfred Thesiger, who loved the desert and spent forty years exploring its inner reaches, including a crossing of Arabia's Empty Quarter. When Teddy Roosevelt decided to explore the River of Doubt in Brazil, he said, "I had to go. It was my last chance to be a boy." It was his passion for adventure that took him to the Amazon, where he picked up the malaria that led to his premature death.

More of late, Arne Rubin, who made the first canoe trip down the Blue Nile; Naomi Uemura, the first to reach the North Pole solo by dogsled; and Robyn Davidson, the first woman to cross the Australian desert by camel, personified this indomitable spirit of exploration, those who followed some irresistible inner call to find *terra incognita,* and the light that illumes the ground within. Always there was healthy risk involved: the catalog is thick with those who didn't come back, from George Leigh Mallory to Amelia Earhart; Ned Gillette, murdered on a glacier in Pakistan; and Doug Gordon, drowned while attempting a first descent of the Tsangpo Gorge in Tibet.

Like all, these adventures needed to be financed. Some used the glossy pretexts of flag planting or coloring in the map and found patrons; others paid their way as journalists, photographers, filmmakers, or shills for commercial products or services. And some had the family pocketbook to underwrite the passion for adventure. One of the first of this class most certainly was the pipe-smoking Englishman Samuel Baker, who spent the early 1860s on a stylish self-financed expedition exploring the watersheds of Abyssinia, camping on Persian rugs beneath double-lined umbrellas as hyenas whooped nearby; a little more than a century later, New Jersey native and self-styled adventurer Joel Fogel financed a first raft descent of the crocodiled lower Omo in Ethiopia with family monies. And the media in recent years have fawned over the various self-financed balloon adventures of doughboys such as Richard Branson.

The stories in this series unpack the minds of men and women who unsuccessfully resisted the temptation to leave the safe harbor, who became inexorably caught in the spiraling steel coils of exploration. Many held a keen conviction that humankind has become too remote from its beginnings, too remote from Nature, too remote from the innocent landscapes that lie within ourselves. The adventures they undertook offered a chance to pluck at the strings of simplicity again, to strip the veneer of dockside worldliness and sail to some more primitive, if more demanding, state of grace; and though the world is sometimes better for the discoveries made in their bold forays, sometimes their searches proved folly, and they didn't come back.

Richard Bangs *is a world adventurer, an award-winning author, and the founder of Mountain Travel Sobek, America's oldest adventure-travel firm. His book* Adventures with Purpose *(Menasha Ridge Press) is a companion to the PBS television series of the same name.*

1/ All Good Gringos Go to Heaven When Shot: Ambrose Bierce

"A man is like a tree: in a forest of his fellows he will grow as straight as his generic and individual nature permits; alone in the open, he yields to the deforming stresses and tortions that environ him."

—Ambrose Bierce, "The Stranger"

A graying gringo wanders the anarchic wilds of northern Mexico. Obstinate streaks of russet hair hint at his Irish ancestry and lend him a temperamental hue that colors his cynical view of the world. He is looking for the legendary Mexican revolutionary Pancho Villa. This is a bold proposition in itself. Does he not realize that any man asking after Villa, even one sympathetic to Villa's revolutionary zeal, could easily be taken for a spy? Even more to the point, does he not realize that his fair skin and American citizenship make this possibility even more likely in the eyes of Villa's defenders—as well as his detractors? After all, this man's own American government would soon come to support one of Villa's rivals. Poking around in this manner could be enough to get anyone killed.

Then again, maybe the tough old gringo ingratiates himself with the young ideologues, and maybe he impresses them with his bravado and his marksmanship. He is a Civil War veteran after all—even sustained a head wound at Kennesaw Mountain. But somewhere during this Mexican campaign, he falls. Is it pneumonia that gets him? Or the more romantic firing squad, the *fusilamiento*?

This is no anonymous man, by the way. This man is a famous writer; now, as he stares down the firing squad, do his own words, from his most famous story, come back to him?

> *Striking through the thought of his dear ones was a sound which he could neither ignore nor understand, a sharp, distinct, metallic percussion like the stroke of a blacksmith's hammer upon the anvil; it had the same ringing quality. He wondered what it was, and whether immeasurably distant or near by—it seemed both. Its recurrence was regular, but as slow as the tolling of a death knell. He awaited each stroke with impatience and—he knew not why—apprehension. The intervals of silence grew progressively longer; the delays became maddening. With their greater infrequency the sounds increased in strength and sharpness. They hurt his ear like the thrust of a knife; he feared he would shriek. What he heard was the ticking of his watch.*

Was this heightened awareness, what one of his own fictional characters had experienced, now happening to him? Was this why he was smiling at the soldiers who stood thirty paces off and held their guns rock steady at his heart? Because he had been right all along, that at the final moments of a man's life, he can feel the very flap of a moth's wing like a screaming gale? Was this why he was smiling? Or was it because this was—in his view—a damned fine way to die, the best way there was?

Imagine if it happened today: a renowned American writer, whose titles include "One of the Missing" and "Mysterious Disappearances," heads off into a lawless frontier and vanishes. What would follow would be a media sensation of epic proportions. Because it happened to Ambrose Bierce in 1914, we know for sure that he is dead. But how it happened, and where his remains lie—these are still, and will probably always be, unanswered questions.

Bierce, most famous in his day for *The Devil's Dictionary* and today for the psychologically realist and oft-anthologized "An Occurrence at Owl Creek Bridge," began life unhappily. He was born on June 24, 1842. His family moved to a farm outside Warsaw, Ohio, when the boy was just four. There, he suffered

Ambrose Bierce

through the relentless chores required by the farmstead and by his stern father, who didn't hesitate to beat the boy mercilessly.

In later years, Bierce wryly referenced the farm in his parody of Samuel Woodworth's 1818 poem "The Old Oaken Bucket," which begins, "How dear to my heart are the scenes of my childhood, / When fond recollection presents them to view! / The orchard, the meadow, the deep tangled wildwood, / And ev'ry loved spot which my infancy knew." Bierce's version: "With what anguish of mind I remember my childhood, / Recalled in the light of a knowledge since gained; / The malarious farm, the wet, fungus grown wildwood, / The chills then contracted that since have remained."

He was gone from this "malarious farm" by age fifteen, working for an antislavery newspaper in Indiana and receiving some schooling at the Kentucky Military Institute. When the Civil War erupted four years later, the adventurous teenager chose sides easily: the north was fighting, in part, to abolish slavery. And while his side eventually won, the war changed him.

With Bierce already on the road to cynicism because of his early experiences on the family farm, the war further deepened the feeling of bitterness he was inclined to hold toward fellow man. (Of course, the bullet lodged in his skull after the campaign in Georgia didn't help matters much, either.) He headed west, to San Francisco, where he eventually got a job as a reporter. There, his cynicism was finely tuned into biting but cogent observations about the world. He could even be described by his own definition of cynic, from his *Devil's Dictionary:* "a blackguard whose faulty vision sees things as they are, not as they ought to be." At his best, Bierce managed to temper his outright disdain for most folks with satire that shone light on other people's absurdities without being overtly mean-spirited. In this way, he can be properly credited as an early influence (and eventual drinking buddy) of H. L. Mencken, easily the twentieth century's most sardonic public wit.

Before he met Mencken, Bierce got a gig writing a column in the *San Francisco Examiner,* a Hearst newspaper. Here, he had the latitude to spit venom at whatever target he liked: often the wealthy, the religious, the politicos—anyone well-heeled and well-connected (even his boss). He earned fame, popularity, and a reputation that led to his nickname: "Bitter Bierce." But Bierce wasn't the type of man who allowed his pen to act as therapist; the inner anguish and anger at the world manifested itself in his relationship with his wife, among others. He wrote: "You are not permitted to kill a woman who has wronged you, but nothing forbids you to reflect that she is growing older every minute. You are avenged fourteen hundred and forty times a day." The better times were those when he went away, which he did often and for weeks at a time. Eventually, despite three children, he and his wife split up, and Bierce entered a bizarre period.

He left the city and took up residence in the woods, living like a hermit, but still writing. During this period, both of his sons died. (A popular story relates an example of Bierce's quirkiness this way: He had one of his sons cremated and kept the ashes. When he remarked about this to Mencken, H. L. said something to the effect of the urn being a sacred spot. Bierce replied that he had no urn; instead, he kept his boy's ashes in a cigar box. Worse, he often opened the box and flicked in the ashes of his own spent cigar to mingle with his progeny's remains.) Of his family, only his daughter, Helen, remained; though she remained loyal to her father, he had trouble completely hiding his disdain for what he saw as her weak intellect.

Increasingly alone and alienated, Bierce, now seventy-one, felt acutely the onset of his twilight. He had always been a person of action, irrepressible and unable to suffer fools. The thought of turning into a doddering old man waiting out his final years was reprehensible to him. At this time, some fifty years after having seen action in the Civil War, the closest and easiest entrée into the action that he craved was just south of the border (and sometimes spilling over it) in Mexico. Pancho Villa's own recruitment posters proclaimed: "We Need you Gringo!! the last adventure it's here! fight in the Mexican Revolution and be proud to ride with Pancho Villa. Viva Villa! Viva la Revolucion!" For a man now in his eighth decade, the allure of a great "last adventure" was too much to ignore. Armed with the fervent belief that a man couldn't possibly report on a war without experiencing it firsthand, he headed toward south Texas, passing through Laredo and venturing west toward the border crossing at El Paso.

There, the story gets murky. But what is indisputable is that he started his journey south from Washington, D.C., in October 1913 and reached northern Mexico by early November. The length of time required for this passage has less to do with the comparatively slow transport of the early twentieth century than with whatever martial demons were haunting Bierce (indeed, had haunted him from the time of his action as a teenager in the Civil War). Heading south, he stopped to visit all the sites of his Civil War battles in Georgia, Tennessee, and Mississippi.

Just before he made his final push toward the border, he consented to an interview with a newsman who remarked that Bierce was dressed from head to toe in black, perhaps "in mourning for the dead over whose battlefields [Mr. Bierce] has been wending his way towards New Orleans." From this observation and the macabre tone of his final letters, it's clear that Bierce was preoccupied with death and dying—he called the chance of never making it out of Mexico alive "possible—even probable." A raging revolutionary war in Mexico would prove a perfect place to illustrate and complement that gloomy mental landscape.

A sense of foreboding and impending demise permeates his last American letters. On September 30: "I am leaving in a day or two for Mexico. If I can get in (and out) I shall go later to South America from some Western port. Doubtless I'm more likely to get in than out, but all good Gringos go to Heaven when shot." A later letter to his niece attempts some softening of what he must have assumed would be his final communication with her. It has an air of solace, but Bierce, being Bierce, couldn't help but allow that solace to be infected with wry despondency: "Good-bye," it begins. "If you hear of my being stood up against a Mexican stone wall and shot to rags please know that I think that a pretty good way to depart this life. It beats old age, disease, or falling down the cellar stairs. To be a Gringo in Mexico—ah, that is euthanasia!"

Most versions of his final weeks have it this way: In El Paso, he crossed the Rio Grande at Ciudad Juárez into Chihuahua State. There, he met up with Villa's army. Villa and Emiliano Zapata led the revolutionary forces against the dictatorship of General Victoriano Huerta. Most accounts have it that Bierce was enthusiastically received. According to Paul Fatout, author of *Ambrose Bierce: The Devil's Lexicographer*, Bierce was "given credentials as an observer attached to Villa's army marching to Chihuahua." Despite the fact that his new credentials were not of a military variety, Bierce took an active role in the Battle of Tierra Blanca, south of Juárez. On this count, Bierce receives a few pages of coverage in University of Chicago historian C. Friedrich Katz's massive 1998 biography, *The Life and Times of Pancho Villa*. Katz recounts the story of a ridiculed Bierce snatching a rifle from some young Mexican soldiers and killing a *federale* from a good distance. The laughing soldiers, thoroughly impressed, presented Bierce with a large sombrero.

So it's clear that things began well. But sometime in the winter of 1913–1914, something went wrong. None of his acquaintances heard from him during most of this period. But on the day after Christmas, Bierce mailed a letter to his secretary back home from the city of Chihuahua. He indicated that he would be riding with Villa's army to the town of Ojinaga, in preparation for an attack. That was the last anyone heard from him; a few weeks into the next year, 1914, he was gone. That is subject to little dispute. But his exact fate has become the subject of much speculation, even today, almost a century later.

There was a battle on January 10 at Ojinaga, not far from the American border. Bierce had already proved his mettle with the killing of the federal soldier; he was, no doubt, emboldened—and encouraged by his young soldier sidekicks—to immerse himself in the heart of the combat. This was a veteran of North America's bloodiest war, after all. And he had come with the express purpose of engaging in one last "great adventure."

The battle at Ojinaga involved an attack on a federal garrison. After Bierce's disappearance, investigators looking for the famous American author interviewed revolutionary soldiers and officers who had been with Bierce at both Chihuahua and Ojinaga. One senior officer testified that in fact he had seen Bierce before the assault at Ojinaga and then had never seen him afterward. So it's logical to conclude that Bierce was killed in battle. Mystery solved. Despite this, there remains the tantalizing proposition, put forth by many, that Bierce was never at Ojinaga at all. In fact, according to this explanation, the entire notion of his going to Mexico was but a ruse, a ploy put forth so that he could exit this life under his own terms and in a location that meant more to him than the barren wastelands of northern Mexico.

Here, the story splits two ways: one west, the other far south.

First, the west: The Grand Canyon was a favorite place of Bierce's. The extraordinary display of one of nature's most awesome spectacles offered itself as an almost irresistible point of departure from this world. Several of Bierce's friends related after his death that he not infrequently uttered that he'd like the Grand Canyon to be his tomb. The theory goes that Bierce never headed to Mexico at all in those last months; instead, he only wrote letters that gave that impression. He did this to throw off those who might not have been respectful of his final wish to die in anonymity in such a cathedral of nature—a place that held illimitable domain over all men and their petty sufferings. At the Grand Canyon, Bierce could stand on a precipitous rim, raise his trusty gun to his head, and allow the bullet to do its work. He would even manage one last smile, one last raise of that ruby mustache before the shot. Then the glorious freefall down the cliff into a land where man didn't tread. It would be the perfect end to a life that had, in Bierce's view, used itself up already.

There are several problems with this surprisingly well-worn supposition. First, of course, there's no body. True, the Grand Canyon can hold many secrets and many bodies (see "The Honeymooners: Glen and Bessie Hyde," Chapter Two). But Bierce disappeared more than ninety years ago. At a minimum, it can be reasonably assumed that if Bierce's end had come this way, his grip would have loosed the gun during his tumble. Even if his body made its way into the Colorado River and washed away forever, some remaining article of his possessions almost certainly would have been found by now. Even more damning is the issue of his final letters. They were posted from northern Mexico, and there were corroborating witnesses to his presence there in those final months of 1913. Of course, it's certainly possible to write letters and have someone else mail them from El Paso and Chihuahua. But this would have required at least one person's complicity, and who was that person? Bierce was a famously isolated man by the end. It's fairly safe to assume that whoever mailed those letters for him would have at least told someone, who then would have told someone else, and so on. Again, in the intervening century, something would have given itself up. This tale of Bierce's demise in the bowels of the Grand Canyon seems to spring mostly from the idea that it would fit a romantic view of Bierce himself and his wishes. It doesn't appear to be rooted in any solid evidence.

The other geographical theory—that he headed even farther south—achieves a bit more currency. While Mexico was a desired destination for Bierce, and he made it clear that he found it probable that he wouldn't return from that country, he also made it clear that, if he had his way, Mexico and its exciting war would be a way station for a locale farther away: South America, which, Bierce once wrote, "held up a beckoning hand to me all my life."

South America earned a reputation through the twentieth century as a continent where people could easily hide. A litany of bootleggers, criminals, and Nazis made places such as Paraguay and Argentina home. Constantly shifting political landscapes, bloody coups, impenetrable jungles, and wide open expanses where what few people there were didn't ask questions made this massive continent a perfect destination for those wishing to flee from a criminal past or, in Bierce's case, the prospect of failing health and final years in the company of those who knew him. To his friends and acquaintances, he was a strong-willed, irascible bugger, and it was a reputation he cherished. Like Hemingway a half century later, Bierce was a man who saw declining physicality as unbearable. To allow people who knew him—and many knew the celebrated author—to see that decline was distasteful to say the least.

Bierce's purported plan to go to South America does allow an easy answer to the issue of his having mailed letters from northern Mexico. Further, the unpredictable nature of war allows for his dying there as well. In fact, he had foreseen it, predicting it several times in his final correspondence sent from America. (Indeed, one can argue that he was so adamant about it that it inspires this question: did he make sure everyone strongly considered the idea of his not coming back because it would then suit him well when in fact he did head to South America and never returned from his stated destination of Mexico?)

While his going to South America—no one seems to know exactly where—isn't entirely farfetched, the stories of what happened to him along the way stretch from unlikely to utterly absurd. One suggests that he never made it to South America, but was captured in the wilds of southern Mexico, where primitive native tribes boiled him alive; his shrunken remains then became objects of tribal idolatry.

If he did make it farther south, differing conjectures include Bierce's hooking up with the famous (some say "infamous") F. A. Mitchell-Hedges, an adventurer and writer who many believe was a British spy. The Brit was sent to Central America to gather information on foreign interests surrounding the Panama Canal. What would have qualified Bierce for such work is anybody's guess. But certainly Bierce would have relished such an adventure—perhaps even more than witnessing a war firsthand. After all, for all his pontificating that a man couldn't hope to write about the ravages of war without seeing them on the battlefield, his experiences in the Civil War scarred him both physically and emotionally. It's not unreasonable to suggest that, contrary to his public statements, hot war was the last thing he wanted to revisit after seeing the battlefields of his youth just a few weeks earlier.

Whatever the case, the story has it that Bierce and Mitchell-Hedges worked their way through Central America, even managing to find a Mayan artifact called the "Skull of Doom" in Guatemala. The Skull of Doom is a replica of a human skull made from pure crystal and is said to hold mystical powers. As with almost everything associated with Mitchell-Hedges, the stories concerning the origin, composition, and acquisition of the skull all have to be weighed against competing assertions and unsubstantiated claims. In any case, not long after getting the skull, Bierce and Mitchell-Hedges are said to have split in British Honduras (modern-day Belize), and Bierce was never seen nor heard from again.

One has to remember that Bierce was a pragmatist who didn't like pompous fools. Indeed, he made a career out of deflating their pomposity. Depending on the camp, Mitchell-Hedges was either a romantic figure— a dashing adventurer hacking his way through impenetrable jungles on his way to making first contact with "uncivilized" tribes and discovering "lost cities," even remnants of Atlantis—or a blowhard, someone capable of spinning fantastic yarns, but given to such overstatement and lapses in truthfulness that he could not be taken at all seriously. For example, in some of his books, he boasts of discovering cities that had been "discovered" long before Mitchell-Hedges was but a notion. Further (though this was long after Bierce's disappearance), Mitchell-Hedges hosted a popular radio program in the 1930s in which he regaled listeners with daring stories of narrow escapes from the hands (and teeth) of jungle-dwelling creatures that would have fit in nicely in the *Princess Bride*'s Fire Swamp. (Of Mitchell-Hedges's book *Land of Wonder and Fear,* the prominent English archaeologist and Mayanist epigrapher Sir John Eric Sidney Thompson wrote, "to me the wonder was how he could write such nonsense and . . . how much taller the next yarn would be.") If Mitchell-Hedges's exploits proved true, such adventures would have thrilled Bierce, but one assumes that he would have tired of Mitchell-Hedges rather quickly. Such grandiosity would have been the very last thing Bierce would have wanted as company for his last great adventure, adventure though it would have been.

As an addendum to this tale, a later Central American explorer claimed that he came across an old, white-haired man clad in animal pelts who was being held by a native tribe that at once revered him as a god and forbade him any movement. Was this Bierce? Or just another in a long line of strange explanations of his fate?

This brings us back to the most likely explanation of what happened to Ambrose Bierce: that he was killed in northern Mexico in early 1914. While the majority of Bierce enthusiasts and historians agree that it was then and there that he met his end, even this story has widely divergent speculations.

The easiest answer, of course, is that he was killed during the war. The most romantic, suggested above, is that he met his end by firing squad after revolutionaries decided that he was asking too many questions about Pancho Villa and took the old gringo to be a spy. More quixotic versions have it that it was Villa himself who killed Bierce, weary of the mocking smart-ass who didn't promise fawning fealty. Or Bierce could have just as easily been killed by federal troops during the attack on the garrison at Ojinaga.

But any of these scenarios raise some questions, most notably: where is the body? No human remains matching Bierce's have ever been found. The Ojinaga battle dead were disposed of, by and large, one of two ways: either they were thrown into mass, unmarked graves, or their bodies were set on fire to avoid typhus outbreaks. Of course, both methods could easily explain why no evidence came to light in the years following Bierce's disappearance and in subsequent investigation by American federal employees. However, later forensic tests failed to turn up anything either.

At least one person claims to have the answer to the question of the body's whereabouts. This man, an American and former priest named James Lienert, believes that Bierce was executed in Sierra Mojada, Mexico, a dusty, end-of-the-road town of fewer than a thousand people in Coahuila State, near the eastern border of Chihuahua State. Lienert so believes the story that he paid to have a memorial plaque installed in the Sierra Mojada cemetery in 2004. It reads:

TESTIGOS MUY CONFIABLES SUPONEN QUE AQUI

YACEN LOS RESTOS DE

1842 AMBROSE GWINNETT BIERCE 1914

FAMOSO ESCRITOR Y PERIODISTA AMERICANO

QUE POR SOSPECHA DE SER ESPIA

FUE FUSLIADO Y SEPTULTADO EN ESTE LUGAR

The English translation: "Very trustworthy witnesses suppose that here / lie the remains of / 1842 Ambrose Gwinnett Bierce 1914 / a famous American writer and journalist / who on suspicion of being a spy / was executed and buried at this place."

Lienert has related the story that once news of the plaque began to circulate in Sierra Mojada, many residents began recalling having heard their parents and grandparents tell about the gringo writer who was executed in town. Why these stories hadn't circulated before the placement of the plaque might have to do with the economic rewards associated with being the home of a still-revered American author. Surely, little else would draw tourists to Sierra Mojada. Modern maps show one faint squiggly line of a road heading in; it's the same route out. Of course, the fact of the town's relative inaccessibility could also easily explain how stories of the old gringo hadn't filtered out before—after all, who would have heard these stories and taken them to the larger world? Lienert, the former priest, is one who did.

As the pastor of Nuestra Señora del Refugio Parish in Sierra Mojada for more than thirty years, Lienert knew the local population intimately. One elderly man he knew was Jesus Benites Avila, also known as Don Chuy. Chuy told Lienert that he remembered a story about an old American who had been drinking with a few soldiers when they went outside to target-shoot. The American went to place the targets. As he did, the soldiers fired on him. The American went down, and as the bullets flew, the man died laughing and smiling.

This certainly sounds like Bierce. It is reasonable, however, to question how it was that Bierce would have even been in federally controlled Coahuila, and especially in Sierra Mojada, some two hundred miles from his last stated destination, Ojinaga. But Lienert felt strongly about the veracity and earnestness of Chuy's recollection. Additionally, Lienert reminds us that traveling to Ojinaga was only Bierce's last "stated intention . . . it does not," in Lienert's words, "state a fact of actually going. The logistics of a campaign are fluid, and subject to quick changes. There could be many reasons for Ambrose altering his intentions. It is not inconceivable that he was asked to go to Sierra Mojada to ascertain the attitudes of the Huertistas, an opposing faction, who were in control of Sierra Mojada at the time."*

At least one source supports the theory of Bierce meeting his end in Sierra Mojada. The American journalist Carey McWilliams's first book, in 1929, was a biography of Bierce. (It was McWilliams who wrote of Bierce, "Obscurity is obscurity, but disappearance is fame.") In his book, McWilliams quotes a cowboy writer, Edward Synott O'Reilly, who claimed that Bierce was buried

*Source: The Ambrose Bierce Site, managed by Don Swaim; www.donswaim.com.

in or near Sierra Mojada after being shot. This claim came from an article that O'Reilly had written for the *New York Times* a year earlier. O'Reilly also wrote an autobiography, titled *Born to Raise Hell*. In it, he wrote that an American had been killed in "Sierra Mohada." Of Bierce, he wrote:

> *Several Mexicans told me about him. They said he was an old man who had come riding in there on horseback, alone . . . He asked questions about the trails and made notes and maps, and they thought he was a spy. When the Federals heard that he was asking how to reach Villa's army they decided to kill him . . . The first shot must have struck him in the leg or belly, because he dropped down, squatting on his heels . . . He squatted there in the dust of the road and began to laugh heartily. The Mexicans were amazed because he was laughing as though it were a tremendous joke that he was being killed.*

If this is true, it makes Chuy's claim a confirmation more than convenient remembrance. All that await now are some forensics tests in that dusty Mexican graveyard.

Recently, the Bierce mystery came into public view once again; "The Devil and Ambrose Bierce," by Jacob Silverstein, was published in *Harper's* in February 2002. Silverstein explains that while working as a reporter for the *Big Bend Sentinel*, a weekly newspaper out of Marfa, Texas, he came across a 1990 letter in an old archive. The author of the letter, Abelardo Sanchez, wrote the following: "Neither Villa nor his men had any involvement in the disappearance of Ambrose Bierce. Bierce died on the night of January 17, 1914, and was buried in a common grave in Marfa the following morning."

Marfa sits at almost five thousand feet elevation in the Trans-Pecos area in southwest Texas. It's more or less a straight line sixty miles south to Ojinaga and the Mexican border. Marfa draws visitors who wish to witness the "Marfa Lights," a series of erratic lights shimmering along the southern horizon. The lights, first recorded some four centuries ago, still manage to elude scientific explanation. The city celebrates its famous luminaries with the Marfa Lights Festival, an annual Labor Day weekend celebration. The revelations brought out by the Silverstein article have not—at least not yet—turned Marfa into a pilgrimage site for Bierce enthusiasts and amateur sleuths.

However, the claims for the Marfa connection certainly appear no less legitimate than any of the other explanations of the author's mysterious disappearance. Sanchez said in his letter to the *Sentinel* that during a drive home to Marfa from California in 1957 (when he was 28 years old), on a Mexican highway, he picked up an elderly hitchhiker named Agapito Montoya who told him that he had been to Marfa many years earlier, "during the Revolution."

As Montoya and four other soldiers fighting against Villa's army in northern Mexico headed south, they came across an old American, alone and afflicted with a bad cold. The old man said he needed help getting across the border and offered the soldiers twenty pesos each if they would help. They agreed, and during the subsequent trip, they found out the following, in Sanchez's words: "[Montoya] heard of different books he [the American] had written including one [Montoya] recalled with the word devil in its title. He said his name in Spanish was Ambrocio [or 'Ambrosia']." During the trip, the man's condition worsened considerably, his cold taking sharp turn toward pneumonia. Because he was so ill and unable to articulate anything, neither the old man nor the soldiers who had ferried him to Marfa were able to secure him any help, and he died soon after. No one in Marfa knew who he was, and when he succumbed to his illness, he was buried in a common grave in town.

Glenn Willeford, a professor at the Center for Big Bend Studies at Sul Ross State University in Alpine, Texas, and an authority on Ambrose Bierce, points out several problems with the Marfa story. In fact, in addition to garnering a myth-busting reference in the Silverstein *Harper's* article, Willeford spends a considerable amount of space debunking the Marfa story in his essay "Ambrose Bierce, 'the Old Gringo': Fact, Fiction and Fantasy," published on www.ojinaga.com. In his essay, Willeford points out the improbability of four soldiers who had just survived a battle with Villa's forces voluntarily turning around for the sum of twenty pesos (equivalent to roughly ten U.S. dollars) to head directly back into the line of danger. The answer, of course, is that maybe they made the calculated decision that their chances for good treatment would increase at the hands of American soldiers if they delivered a dying American to them. But Willeford counters that Montoya's story doesn't indicate that they ever sought such favored treatment. However, it should be noted that, if Sanchez's story is true, Montoya said that the soldiers simply didn't have the English to persuade the Americans, and that their quarry was incapacitated and couldn't communicate his identity either.

But Willeford points out something else: it's a decent bet that among the many American soldiers and the gaggle of American newspapermen milling about the area at the time, at least one of them would have recognized Bierce; though this was before television would have transmitted his image coast to coast, Bierce was a famous man. Even if no one recognized him, certainly an old, dying American would have stood out among the other victims in and around Marfa; the rest were by and large young Mexicans. Further, extensive searches into the records of the Presidio County Courthouse failed to turn up any reference to a Bierce, or any unidentified older American, having died in or near Marfa during that period.

The bottom line is that all these divergent theories persist simply because no trace of Bierce has ever turned up. After all these years, the famous writer's disappearance still keeps its secrets. It's most likely that Bierce did in fact make his trip to Mexico—too many pieces of evidence exist to suggest otherwise—with the intention of heading to South America once he got his fill of action. He probably never made it out of Mexico. But what exactly were the circumstances that surrounded that failure to leave? That's the question that doggedly refuses an easy answer.

Bierce's disappearance isn't simply grist for amateur historians and literature enthusiasts. While many modern Americans perhaps possess only a fleeting familiarity with Bierce's name (or no familiarity at all), he does still inspire modern interpretation and consideration. The famous Mexican writer Carlos Fuentes published *The Old Gringo* in 1985. The novel sees Bierce as the central actor in the story's landscape. The book has the interesting distinction of being the first American best seller written by a Mexican author. In 1989, a movie version, *Old Gringo,* was made, starring Jane Fonda, Jimmy Smits, and, as Ambrose Bierce, Gregory Peck.

Though the movie is coming on twenty years of age and the book has already passed that milestone, I had my own bizarre run-in with the Bierce legend relatively recently.

In 2002, on a trip to visit my sister's family in San Antonio, Texas, my brother Erik and I decided to wake before dawn, hop in the rental car, and head down I-35 to Mexico. It's a straight shot down the interstate to Laredo and across the International Bridge to Nuevo Laredo, Mexico, where things look pretty much the same as in Laredo, but tend to cost half as much.

Erik lives in Atlanta, and I live in Baltimore. These are pretty populated areas where, whether you like it or not, you're going to pass a multitude of places to stop and eat, shop, or relieve yourself. This is our reality, and so it didn't occur to us that we didn't stand much of a chance of finding anything along a major interstate on the way to the border. It's a decent trip—three hours or so. (We hovered around 65 mph. My brother-in-law told me that south of San Antonio "might as well be called 'northern Mexico' for all its difference"; something about that image made Erik and me obey all posted speed limits.) We had set off without breakfast, planning to grab a quick bite somewhere south of San Antonio.

"Somewhere south of San Antonio": vast scrubland monotonously spreading out from the asphalt into a hazy horizon of unattractive scrub and sky. The uniformity was broken only by an occasional soulless, tin-roofed shack with requisite automobile carcass shining in the brutal sun. An hour south of San Antonio, Erik irritably mentioned that his stomach was digesting itself. I mumbled something in response about the beauty of the lightening sky. Truth was, it revealed only more wasteland, and nothing beautiful besides. Anyway, I was more concentrated on an impending intestinal requirement.

Finally, somewhere between Cotulla (population 3,500) and Encinal (population a lot, lot less), we saw a roadside flophouse appear almost like a mirage. It had a single gas pump out front with an "out of order" sign attached to it. A sign reading simply "Eat" hung above the doorway. We skidded into the parking area—indistinguishable from the scrub beyond—and approached the door with the caution of burglars staking out a suburban window. I'm not precisely sure why, but we both regarded the situation as if we believed that what awaited us was as likely the lip of a rifle as a grease-spattered spatula.

Fortunately, it was the spatula, and a matching grease-spattered apron as well. "Come in, come in," bellowed a tall, thin man with black hair and mustache. A name tag that read "Kendall" hung precariously from his apron. "I'm running all over," he said, his arms and legs moving as if he were a marionette. "My girls [the waitresses, he would later tell us] all called in hung over. I've said it before, but this is the last time we do payday on Friday nights. So I'm running the place myself."

I couldn't see what the frenzy was about. We were the only people there. I asked where the bathroom was, and he produced a key and told me to go to the building next door—a motel, as best I could figure out. On my way out, I gave Erik a glance, taking in what he was wearing should I have to give a description to the police.

But when I returned, not only was he still in the spot where I had left him, but also orange juice sat under his nose, a steaming mug of coffee sat near my place at the table, and Ken, appendages crooked over every corner of his chair, sat talking to Erik. He turned to me and explained that breakfast was on the grill and would be up shortly. While I sat down and sipped the black coffee, Erik was wrapping up an explanation of what he did for a living and where he did it. "At-a-lanta," Ken exclaimed. "Hot-lanta!" he said, and threw his head back. We waited for a story, some connection to the place, but instead an uncomfortable silence ensued while Ken looked at us both.

Erik and I are the sons of New Yorkers; long silences fill us with discomfort. I am absolutely unable to handle them, and I often wind up blurting out anything to fill the space.

"I don't live in Atlanta," I said, on cue. "I'm in Baltimore. The Falcons suck," I added, completely unsure why I had said it or even where that rejoinder had come from.

"Yeah," Ken managed, obviously as confused by my outburst as I was. "What do you do?" he asked.

"I teach."

"Yeah? What grade?"

"College."

"What subject?"

"English," I said, lowering my lips to my mug. What followed made me perk my eyebrows, helped by the strong coffee.

"You heard of Ambrose Bierce?" he asked.

Sure, I knew of Ambrose Bierce. Every semester in one of my lit classes, I torture my students with "An Occurrence at Owl Creek Bridge." Most of them say they didn't understand it, but the more perceptive among them begrudgingly mumble, "That was pretty cool," or allow, "It didn't totally suck," a not-so-veiled reference to the fact that they think my other choices for the semester's reading do, in fact, suck.

"I know where he's buried," Ken said. "Hold on." He ran behind the counter.

At the time, all I knew was that Bierce had disappeared somewhere along the Mexico-Texas border, but that it was far west of where we were then—at least I thought so. I whispered as much to Erik.

"But it could be close, right?" he offered. I didn't have a map in front of me, but I knew that West Texas was massive, easily able to encompass my Maryland. "I don't think so," I replied, "but who knows?"

Ken returned with three large plates brimming with eggs, toast, grits, and sausage. He balanced the plates, one resting its lip on the next like an unfurled accordion, up his left arm. With his right hand, he administered the plates at three spots and sat down to eat with us.

Ken shoveled in bites of toast and began the story: "You know, when Ambrose came down here after seeing where he fought in the Civil War, he went through San Antonio."

I smiled; I loved the way Ken had referred to the author as "Ambrose," as if he and the author were old buddies.

"Then Ambrose came down this very way you two did. No interstate then, of course, but the same route. Headed straight for the border at Laredo and crossed into Mexico at Nuevo Laredo. The old story goes that he heard all the action was over in Chihuahua, so he went west to El Paso to cross there instead of down here at Laredo. But the truth is, Ambrose got all mixed up with officers from Fort Sam Houston and because they were far enough away from the action, they spent days getting piss drunk and visiting brothels all up and down southern Texas from San Antonio to Laredo."

(While researching this book, I discovered that Ken's story, at least to this point, isn't at all far-fetched. Two Bierce biographers, Paul Fatout [*Ambrose Bierce: The Devil's Lexicographer*, 1951] and Roy Morris, Jr. [*Ambrose Bierce: Alone in Bad Company*, 1995], confirmed that Bierce, on his way to Mexico, stopped at Fort Sam Houston in San Antonio and met up with old military buddies from years earlier. According to Fatout, Bierce was "royally entertained by Fort Sam Houston cavalry officers." Morris adds, "The officers of the Third Cavalry treated him like a foreign ambassador and could hardly be dissuaded from parading the regiment in his honor." All of this I would learn later—when I would come to regard Ken with a little less suspicion. But at that roadside eatery between San Antonio and Laredo, I was, admittedly, a lot more incredulous.)

In the restaurant, I raised my eyebrows and glanced at Erik. We were in the midst of the very route that Ken told us Bierce and the officers had traveled to do their carousing, and it sure looked to us as if there wasn't a damn thing around. Could there have been that many places to visit some ninety years earlier? Of course this wasn't central Maryland, where there generally isn't a history of whole towns booming and then withering away from bust years later. Things were, I had to admit, different around here. I asked Ken to go on.

"Well, Ambrose got sick. Just a cold at first, but then it turned into an infection—bronchitis, then pneumonia. He got real ill, but he kept on drinking and partying. Then he died during the night while all the guys were sleeping off a real bender around a campfire just around here." Ken swept his arm around the establishment, indicating, it looked to me, that the great Ambrose Bierce was buried just behind the counter leading to the kitchen.

"Why didn't they take him back home to be buried?" Erik asked.

Ken sipped his coffee. He had an air of confidence—an absence of hysterical need to convince us that everything he was saying was true—that made this explanation seem perfectly reasonable. "Two reasons," he said. "First, Ambrose wanted to go to Mexico to see the war. If the soldiers sent him back home, he would have failed. And they would have been responsible. And that's the other part of it. They *were* responsible. This guy was almost eighty years old [seventy-one, really], and they had him out at night partying and drinking, even after he got sick. It was December, remember. It gets cold at night. These guys probably felt like they killed him. Ambrose was loved back at the fort. How could they go back and tell everyone that he died while they slept right next to him? It was easier to let the story continue that he went on to Mexico. They even wrote up some letters and had them mailed later from Mexico, so it would look like he was there."

In retrospect, this part seems implausible, but I didn't know as much at the time. It all actually sounded somewhat reasonable—hell, it isn't any more unreasonable than the other theories out there. "So where's his body now?" I asked Ken.

"Somewhere around here. It's pretty easy to keep a body hid here for a long time without anyone disturbing it. Even if someone did dig it up to build something, would they really go to the effort of trying to find out who some old bones belonged to? No, Ambrose rests peacefully somewhere between San Antonio and Laredo. Could be in my very backyard. I don't know."

I thought to ask Ken how he knew all this, but that seemed beside the point. Even now, as I write this book, it still seems somewhat beside the point. The larger issue, I suppose, is that Ambrose Bierce lives on in the imaginations of many people. Even those who run roadside flophouses along a lonely stretch of highway carrying two visitors toward the Mexican border, following a route that Ambrose Bierce himself took—*probably* took.

2/ No Fear of Failure: Percy Fawcett

How many chances do we get? How many measures of space between a naked toe and the lightning strike of snake fang, spider pincer, or scorpion tail? How many rivers can we wade stocked with flesh-hungry piranha? How many jungle diseases hover by, ready to enter our delicate urban systems?

If we escape all these things, how also do we escape encounters with natives who assume of us the worst?

Three men make their way through the jungle. One hobbles along on a foot badly infected, skin falling off in chunks. Legions of flies descend on the men, madden them until they sit on the brink of lunacy. The flies are a nuisance, but one that must be tolerated. But add to them the bees and the mosquitoes above, the ticks and biting ants below. Whole squadrons darken the skies in black clouds; the ground itself moves in concert with the swarms. There is an incessant battle, any bit of exposed flesh smacked at constantly, all points on the body continually swatted at, plucked, slapped, in an effort to find some relief.

The war with the insects becomes so intense that it's easy to lose one's way. But one must remain alert, attuned to everything. After all, this is also the land of the venomous snake, the poisonous spider, flesh-eating fish, and burrowing parasites. And if this war with the natural world and its riot of stinging, biting, killing creatures isn't enough, humans here are simply part of the landscape, animal like any other—except possessing more advanced weaponry. Was it a band of these humans that the three Englishmen stumbled on? Did these Indians, bows pulled taut, mean the demise of the explorers?

"You need have no fear of any failure . . ." Those were the last words anyone ever received from the leader of these three men; none of them were ever seen again. He was also the author of the following words:

> *At least once in every man's lifetime death looks him straight in the eyes—and passes on. In forest travel it is never far off. It shows itself in many aspects, most of them horrible, but some apparently so innocuous that they scarcely win attention, though none the less deadly for that. Time and time again the concatenation of events leads up to the very edge of disaster, and halts there. The flight of an arrow—an inch of space—a moment of time—on such insignificant details does fate hang.*

The author of such hopeful words understood, of course, the flip side of this: the inch could shrink to a centimeter, to a millimeter, to no space at all, until the deadly object finds purchase in the bosom of the now-dead man.

The understanding of this breeds a healthy fear. It's a peculiar type of fear: one born of recognition. The man has been through all this before. There's nothing new under the forest canopy—no insect, no snake, no feline predator, no pointy tip of arrow ready to be let go, to find its mark deep in one's rib cage. He's seen it all. And because of this, precisely because he has lived through it all before, calm in the face of such danger, utterly composed despite hardships that have broken lesser men, he stands and waits, his arms half-raised in a gesture of calm to his two green companions.

This is most probably the final scene.

Percy Harrison Fawcett, a man nearing his seventh decade of life, set off into uncharted lands deep in the Brazilian Mato Grosso, a massive wilderness of swamp full of snakes, insects, and unreceptive Indians, in search of a legendary lost city, a place he dubbed simply "Z." This man also had an interest in the occult and parallel modes of discovery, such as psychometry. It's easy to dismiss such a man as a dreamer, totally detached from reality. Or perhaps a crass opportunist, out only for gold and advancement. But that man once wrote the

Percy Fawcett

following words, just before embarking on the journey from which he would never return:

> *If the journey is not successful my work in South America ends in failure, for I can never do any more. I must inevitably be discredited as a visionary, and branded as one who had only personal enrichment in view. Who will ever understand that I want no glory from it—no money for myself—that I am doing it unpaid in the hope that its ultimate benefit to mankind will justify the years spent in the quest?*

Percy Fawcett was born in 1867 in Devon, England. His father was a fellow of the Royal Geographic Society (RGS), fitting for a man who would bear a son whose very life was the definition of adventure. In the British military, Percy Fawcett drew posts to such exotic locales as Ceylon (today's Sri Lanka) and North Africa. During these stints, he learned surveying, a skill that would one day take him much farther afield.

Indeed, in 1906, the RGS (whose impressive roster of members has included Richard Burton, Charles Darwin, John Hope Franklin, Edmund

Hillary, David Livingstone, Ernest Shackleton, and Henry Morton Stanley, among others) sent Fawcett to survey jungle areas straddling the Bolivian and Brazilian borders. The massive blank spots on the society's maps proved an irresistible lure for Fawcett. The governments of both countries, eager to exploit the growing rubber wealth there, wanted an impartial judge to set the boundaries. The president of the RGS, upon presenting the case to Fawcett, remarked, "One hears the most appalling tales of this rubber country. Then there's the risk of disease—it's rife everywhere. It's no use trying to paint an attractive picture . . ." Despite the promised hardships of such a job, Fawcett accepted without hesitation. In fact, nothing could have dissuaded him. He later wrote, "There were my wife and son to consider, and another child on the way; but Destiny intended me to go, so there could be no other answer." Ultimately, his delimitation work created boundary lines that still exist today.

On that first expedition, Fawcett was presented with a startling reality that would have turned off lesser men to the job ahead. The warnings back in England all centered on the suffocating heat and humidity of the jungle, with its assortment of biting insects, killer snakes and animals, and hostile native tribes. But setting off from La Paz, Fawcett and his party first had to climb to seventeen thousand feet in the Andes, a labor that taxed men and pack animals alike. Nights were freezing, and while the magnificent views would be enough to sustain anyone ("I was crushed by the grandeur—speechless with the overpowering wonder of it!" Fawcett wrote), one false step off a precipitous ledge while admiring those views meant certain death—all this before the party even reached the jungle. This would be an adventure indeed, but it would be no pleasure cruise.

His accounts of the expedition (and all subsequent ones) included tales of hearty men dying of disease and accident, and of privations that sent even those initially gung-ho into absolute tizzies, soothed only by copious drink. Nevertheless, Fawcett thrived—and without the drink. While men and animals fell off one by one, Fawcett kept on, seemingly impervious to the ills around him—or possessing that famous British reserve and penchant for understatement characteristic of all the famous British explorers of the nineteenth and twentieth centuries.

Whatever the hardships, Fawcett soldiered on, driven by the excitement and novelty of it all, for this was truly a land apart. The rivers in the Bolivian Montana, as the forested region was called, "were in fact more remote from La Paz than was England." If measured in actual miles, this is a great exaggeration, but in terms of literal time of travel, the statement was both accurate and startling. "The remoteness of a place such as Riberalta [in the Bolivian jungle] is difficult to grasp. There was no telegraph or other communication with La Paz, or any other place, and under the most favourable conditions the capital was two-and-a-half months' journey distant," Fawcett wrote.

Because of the area's inaccessibility, Fawcett had no choice but to quickly learn the ways of jungle travel and all its attendant problems; these would serve him well in subsequent travels. For example, of monkeys, he wrote, "Their meat tastes rather pleasant; but at first the idea revolted me because when stretched over a fire to burn off the hair they looked so horribly human. The newcomer has to become hardened to these things and leave his fastidiousness behind him—or else starve." And starve he nearly did, later. But the jungle wasn't the only hazard; Indians could be hostile and cannibalistic. And many of the Europeans living in the jungle profiting from the rubber boom presented danger as well. Fawcett once told of an *intendente* in a Bolivian *barraca* who drew his sword on a subaltern. Fawcett stepped between them and then faced a revolver held in a hand unsteadied by alcohol. Fawcett wrestled the gun away while others grabbed the *intendente* and dragged him off.

What amazes one about Percy Fawcett is that in the midst of so many lawless, squalid, remote, and dangerous lands, he never seems to lose his civilized edge, and perhaps more amazing for a man in his Victorian times, he rarely casts a condescending eye or verbal sneer at those very elements. Fawcett was no hypocrite, condemning the barbarism of others while singing the virtues of his own civilized, beloved British or his European compatriots: "Responsible for the taming of the West African colonies, we ourselves are in no position to throw stones. To cry out at the atrocities of the rubber boom, while saying nothing of the many cruelties still legally sanctioned in our own country safe out of the public's sight, is to be too narrow in outlook. I must again stress that what took place in Bolivia and Peru was not sanctioned by their Governments, but was the act of individuals outside the range of law and order. Bad as it was, nothing occurred there comparable with the atrocities in the Belgian Congo." Understanding the damning influence of European conquest in the Americas and elsewhere, Fawcett had a soft spot for the "uncivilized" Indians he encountered: "My experience is that few of these savages are naturally 'bad,' unless contact with 'savages' from the outside world had made them so."

Of course, raiding parties designed to bring in slaves for the booming rubber plantations gave the Indians every reason for hostility, if they hadn't been previously disposed that way. Fawcett was appalled at the treatment the natives received and made it a practice that he would never come to native tribes with malice, believing that if treated with dignity and respect, the native would return the favor. The result was that Fawcett many times faced down very hostile natives with only raised hands in offering. Usually other members of his party cowered behind in the bushes, revolvers at the ready. In one famous episode, Fawcett ordered the men of his party to withstand a fusillade of arrows while they played the banjo and accordion and belted out "Swanee River" and "A Bicycle Built for Two." The stunned natives accepted the serenade as an act of friendship, and good relations were established. And though a teetotaler himself, Fawcett even had sympathy for those "sodden with drink," understanding that in such squalid, isolated places, alcohol provided the only reasonable escape.

As Fawcett made more and more expeditions, he even came to view the peculiar offenses of jungle travel with amusement. On a filthy, run-down boat, slung in a hammock, he observed, "At night the rats on board . . . mustered in regiments, held a gymkhana on deck, swarmed up the stays, ran along our hammock ropes, and chased one another over our bodies. In the light of early morning I woke to see two sitting on my stomach calmly washing their faces." But even with humor intact, nothing could completely paper over the difficulties he and his crews faced. They were even once detained as prisoners of war in a Brazilian river port before being allowed to proceed no worse for wear.

After Fawcett completed his work in Bolivia and handed over his maps and papers to the Bolivian president, he was asked if he would lead another expedition, this time delimiting the border with Brazil along the River Paraguay. Despite the difficulties of the expedition he had just been through, he snapped up the opportunity. But he would go back to England first. He wrote, "Ahead of me was the glorious prospect of home. For the present I was satiated with the wild, and my mind was full of the coming journey to the coast; of the lazy sea voyage, and the sight of England, with its funny little trees, neat fields, and fairy-tale villages; of my wife, the four-year-old Jack, and the latest arrival, Brian. I wanted to forget atrocities, to put slavery, murder and horrible disease behind me, and to look again at respectable old ladies whose ideas of vice ended with the indiscretions of so-and-so's housemaid."

The true adventurer knows this: home and blessed routine, silence and safety—these are the greatest things in the world. But soon enough, they bore one to tears. Percy Fawcett would be back to the jungle before long. Safe back home in England for only a short time, Fawcett knew it: "A nostalgic pang shot through me. Inexplicably—amazingly—I knew I loved that hell. Its fiendish grasp had captured me, and I wanted to see it again."

Over the next twenty years, he would go back to South America on eight different expeditions, covering vast swaths of the middle of the continent from the Pacific to the Atlantic. South America had him in its grip and, with the tenacity of an anaconda, wouldn't let go.

Back in Bolivia for his next expedition, Fawcett's party found the source of the River Verde. His findings corrected mistaken guesses made in 1873. The result was an additional 1,200 square miles for Bolivia; the government was, of course, thrilled. The party had been a great success.

A survey of the border along the Peruvian side, along the Madre de Dios and Heath rivers, meant yet another expedition. There came a brief interlude back home in England. Once again, the same "nostalgic pang" for the jungle was quick to arrive: "[A]fter a month or two, thoughts of the wild places—with all their pests and diseases, their misery and discomfort—disturbed the ambient peace and called me back. I would leave, heartsick at another long parting from the home circle, yet deep down inside me something was exulting at the escape from everyday life!" Fawcett, upon heading back to the jungle, would surround himself with men of his ilk, one of them exclaiming upon return: "It's hell all right, but one kind of likes it!"

Fawcett wrote of his adventures on these expeditions, but left the great manuscript unfinished. As his son Brian, who compiled his father's writings into the volume *Lost Trails, Lost Cities* (1953), wrote: "There remained a finale to be added later—the great climax which his last expedition should have supplied. But the forest, in allowing him a peep at its soul, claimed his life in payment. The pages he had written in the confidence of a sure achievement became part of the pathetic relics of a disaster whose nature we had no means of knowing."

It was the subject of lost civilizations that always interested Fawcett. He was driven by the search for new knowledge. In the remotest jungles of South America, such a thing wasn't hard to find—this was, after all, the first two decades of the twentieth century, before American and European universities had entire departments of cultural anthropology. Far below the surface of these strange and sometimes terrible lands, it was entirely conceivable that the remnants of past civilizations were just waiting to be discovered. That such cities still existed was an idea of great currency in the highest reaches of

Brazilian intellectual society in the early twentieth century. Fawcett, already intimately familiar with the landscape and the dangers that lay in the way, was the perfect man to go searching for these cities. But it wasn't only Fawcett's accomplishments in surveying and experience in the jungle that made him the ideal candidate. He was also someone for whom the personal glories attached to such a triumph of discovery were unimportant. "What can be more enthralling than penetration into the secrets of the past," he once wrote, "and throwing light upon the history of civilization itself?"

Brazil's Mato Grosso was the perfect hiding place for such a city—so remote as to be itself a lost world, unexplored, large swaths completely uninhabited. Had it always been that way? No one seemed to know for sure. Scraps of information gleaned from Indians, rubber traders, and explorers formed a cogent idea that a lost city might exist in that region.

Discussing the possibility with a British consul, Fawcett was told that the northern regions of the Mato Grosso had never been entered. The consul added, "Mark my words: it'll never be explored on foot, however big and well-equipped the expeditions. Possibly, in a hundred years' time, flying machines will do it—who knows?"

That proclamation proved a challenge too tempting to ignore. But it also must be remembered that Fawcett was no delusional dreamer possessing outsize visions without any grounding in reality. He knew how stories could grow into legends and how simple facts could take on the specter of fantasy. In his writings, Fawcett tells of the time when his party, in its effort to shed excess weight, buried, among other items, sixty pounds worth of gold. In subsequent years, tales of this hidden treasure inflated the holdings to sixty thousand pounds, and, "Of course, the glowing accounts make no mention of the fact that we retrieved the buried equipment later. Let the would-be treasure-hunter ponder on the moral of this tale!"

But there were simply too many corroborated stories of lost cities and civilizations spread out through the massive forested regions of the continent to be ignored. Certainly the recent discovery of the ancient Incan wonderland at Machu Picchu lent much credence to this idea. The Spaniards had been traipsing all over these lands for centuries without discovering it. And all the Indian tribes nearby spoke of a more ancient civilization than the Incas. There were animals still unknown to science in those regions (as there are even now in the twenty-first century), so why not hidden human civilizations as well? Indeed, many anthropologists still speak of tribes deep in those regions completely untouched by white men.

Few, even in hindsight, would find fault in any of these conjectures about lost cities. Where Fawcett gets in trouble in the posterity game is not his belief in lost cities, but his other beliefs in parallel universes, psychometrics, theosophy, and similar philosophical and mystical ideas. Fawcett grounded his convictions about a lost city partly in the claims of a psychic he had consulted, Margaret Lumley Brown (who wrote under the pen name "Irene Hay"), who had visions of an ancient continent stretching across the present-day Atlantic from north Africa to South America. This continent was submerged by a cataclysmic event (taking Atlantis with it), and the remnants were pushed into modern-day South America, constituting evidence of an ancient and advanced race. The members of this race were fair-skinned and had an aptitude for making themselves disappear when approached. Their homeland—which Fawcett dubbed "Z"—would be his destination.

Fawcett also possessed a black stone idol that, he claimed, escaped conclusive hypotheses from any scientists as to its origin and meaning. Fawcett wrote, "I could think of only one way of learning the secret of the stone image, and that was by means of psychometry—a method that may evoke scorn by many people but is widely accepted by others who have managed to keep their minds free from prejudice."

In Fawcett's communication with Lumley Brown, he indicated his beliefs about the lost city of Z. The psychic's response only encouraged Fawcett: "Your query suggests that you have been getting communications purporting to be of an Atlantean nature. Such is not impossible as Atlantis is very much 'in the air' just now. Such communication might certainly come through sensitives; that is to say waves of released information are picked up, or a deliberate plan is being developed."

There was also the story of a powerful tribe of Musus (Brazilian Toltecs) who subjugated rival tribes and set them up in a circular fashion around the Musus' city, ordering them to kill all who attempted trespass. Over centuries, this tribe supposedly became isolated from all others. But its legend grew, and those who managed to penetrate the defenses and convince the tribe of friendliness came back with great treasures.

Fawcett speculated that these two divergent theories could actually be one and the same story—this race of isolated people, encircled by once-hostile tribes. In the case of the Atlantean ancestors, the protectorate tribes were the Morcegos Indians, who lived in rattan-covered caves. Area tribes spoke of the Morcegos—called "bats" because they liked to come out only at night— alternatively as if they could have disappeared thousands of years ago or as if they still inhabited the deepest regions of the Mato Grosso. This, too, was not at all unreasonable.

Many of the inland tribes of the Amazon had a sense of time that didn't correspond to our own: they would tell stories of "yesterday" that occurred a hundred years earlier. But Fawcett points out something worth remembering: "The 11,000 years said by Plato to have passed since the last of the Atlantean islands submerged could be spanned by the lifetime of only 110 centenarians. An eye-witness account of the disaster could be passed on from father to son down to the present day with only 184 repetitions!"

Sure, Fawcett was a dreamer, but one who tempered wild visions with a true critical eye and oodles of experience. So he would set off to the fabled city Z. But first he had to raise the necessary funds, no easy task.

"Men of science had in their day pooh-poohed the existence of the Americas," Fawcett wrote. "And, after, the idea of Herculaneum, Pompeii and Troy. You might argue that those great discoveries had confounded the incredulous, and this should have been in my favor. As a Founder's Medallist of the Royal Geographic Society I was accorded a respectful hearing, but to get the elderly gentlemen or the archaeologists and museum experts in London to credit a fraction of what I knew to be true was a task altogether beyond my powers."

Despite his accomplishments, Fawcett's theory of an ancient cataclysm was too much for the powers that be. But Fawcett was undeterred. Before setting off, he relayed the requisite belief in the unbelievable that any true explorer must possess: "I have probed from three sides for the surest way in; I have seen enough to make any risk worth while in order to see more, and our story when we return from the next expedition may thrill the world!"

Late in 1924, Fawcett went to New York to secure funding for the expedition; it would come from private sources, and not from government or science organizations. He agreed to sell all newspaper rights to the expedition to the North American Newspaper Alliance.

In February 1925, Percy Fawcett, his son Jack, and Jack's friend Raleigh Rimell set out from England for Rio de Janeiro and then São Paulo. Things began well, though a bit too slowly for Jack's anxious tastes. Through the month and into March, they made their way interminably deeper into the jungle. There was an insufferable period of eight days aboard a crowded steamer on the

Paraguay, São Laurenco, and Cuyaba rivers. Over the next month and a half, the team traveled to the remote outpost at Bacairy.

The party's first objective was Dead Horse Camp, so named because that is where Fawcett's horse had died on an expedition in 1921. Their intended route thereafter would take them northeast along the Xingu River to "The Stone Tower," an edifice that, according to legend, was somehow illuminated by a never-extinguished light. Fawcett described it thus: "There are rumors . . . of a strange source of light in the buildings, a phenomenon that filled with terror the Indians who claimed to have seen it." From the Stone Tower, it was an almost straight shot east to Z. From there, a southeast route would take them across the São Francisco River to a fabled city of tremendous wealth written of by a Portuguese explorer in 1753. From there, it was a relatively easy trek out of the jungle through the villages of Xiquexique and Lencois to the coastal city of Bahia, where they could get a steamer home.

In late May, the party did indeed reach Dead Horse Camp. Here, in a letter to his wife, Fawcett described the miserable conditions created by the relentless insects. He recounted the condition of the team: Jack was doing splendidly; Rimell was suffering badly with an infected foot; and as for himself: "Years tell, in spite of the spirit of enthusiasm." Of Dead Horse Camp, and of his old companion, Fawcett wrote, "Only his white bones remain . . . It is *very cold* at night, and fresh in the morning; but heat and insects come by mid-day, and from then till six o'clock in the evening it is sheer misery in camp."

And then, Fawcett's last recorded words: "You need have no fear of failure." None of the three men were ever heard from again.

Some claimed that Fawcett's disappearance was intentional, seizing on sentiments he often expressed:

> *It seems that one is destined to meet with Englishmen even in the most isolated places in South America . . . in many ways they are to be envied. Their standing in the community is considerable, and they live easily and in a fair degree of comfort, and there are few worries to distract them. Their existence provides sure escape from the lurking fear of that heritage of worn-out financial system—unemployment.*

I believe the attraction is more in this than anything else. The English peel off the unessentials of modernity very easily—they 'go native' more readily than any Europeans except the Italians; and the more refined their upbringing the quicker the change comes about. There is no disgrace in it. On the contrary, in my opinion, it shows a creditable regard for the real things of life at the expense of the artificial . . . it is not uncommon to find that the utmost simplicity in living is sought for its own sake.

Even as Fawcett made his way toward his final destination, he echoed this sentiment: "This part of the country [in the Mato Grosso] is so beautiful that I could well understand why, scattered through the forests, there are hermits of many nationalities, preferring a life alone in the wild to a penurious and uncertain existence in civilization. Rather than pity them for losing the amenities we are accustomed to consider so necessary, we should envy them for having the wisdom of knowing how superfluous such things really are. Perhaps they are the ones most likely to find the true meaning of life."

True, the lure of the wild, the simplicity one can enjoy there, was probably always prominent for Percy Fawcett. But here was a man who subscribed to a high moral code and for whom family (despite Fawcett's penchant for leaving his for months, even years, at a time) was sacrosanct. It is very unlikely that he would willingly go off into the jungle and leave his wife forever—more unlikely still that he would commit his son to that as well. He knew well the hardships his long absences had caused his family: "My wife and children have been . . . denied many of the benefits that they would have enjoyed had I remained in the ordinary walks of life. Of our twenty-four years of married life only ten have been spent together . . . yet my wife has never complained. On the contrary, her practical help and constant encouragement have been big factors in the successes so far granted, and in the end the triumph will be largely due to her." It is doubtful that he would walk into the jungle without the intention of returning home. Further, at the beginning of the expedition, Jack Fawcett wrote in a letter to his brother Brian: "When Raleigh and I are unusually fed up [with waiting to get farther into the jungle] we talk of what we will do when we revisit Seaton in the spring of 1927, with plenty of cash. We intend to buy motor-cycles and really enjoy a good holiday in Devon, looking up all our friends and visiting the old haunts." If it indeed was Fawcett's intention to "go native," he either had Jack's complicity or had kept the terrible truth hidden from his son. Both scenarios are quite improbable.

More likely is the simple and credible motive that Fawcett always maintained: there were lost cities out there, and the discovery of them would advance science and human knowledge. Fawcett had survived many expeditions to places where even natives broke down and succumbed to the elements. Further, he had something to prove; he *knew* there were cities out there. And this can be said without hyperbole: there was probably no man on earth more qualified to know. Fawcett had "traveled much in places not familiar to the other explorers, and the wild Indians have again and again told me of the buildings, the character of the people, and the strange things beyond."

Despite this, Percy and Jack Fawcett and Raleigh Rimell had disappeared.

Hampering the prospects of search efforts was the fact that Fawcett was deliberately vague about the specifics of his final expedition; instead, he gave only a broad outline of his party's projected route, partly to protect would-be rescuers. "If we should not come out, I don't want rescue parties to come in looking for us," he wrote. "It's too risky. If with all my experience we can't make it, there's not much hope for others. That's one reason I'm not telling exactly where we're going."

In 1927, a French civil engineer named Roger Courteville claimed that he had met a tattered, older white man who said he was Fawcett in the Brazilian state of Minas Gerais. But in the end, no one could persuade the North American Newspaper Alliance to part with the funds necessary to go back, and Courteville's claim could never be verified. The first official search party didn't set out until 1928, three years after the three men disappeared. The alliance finally sent a party led by George Dyott, who concluded that Fawcett and the others had been killed by hostile Indian tribes.

A Swiss trapper named Stefan Rattin later managed an interview with a European man being held captive in a remote Indian encampment. The man was in dire straits and muttered something about his "sleeping son." The veracity of this account wasn't questioned; however, the Swiss trapper described the old man (who never gave his name) in very specific physical terms, including eye color and approximate height, which did not match Percy Fawcett's appearance.

That there was a white captive was well within the realm of possibility. Indian tribes often took prisoners, eager to make use of their "prize," a person who carried clothing and metal instruments. The captive could be paraded as something to show off to rival tribes. So, when journalist and historian Harold Wilkins wrote some twenty years after Fawcett's disappearance that he might still be alive, it wasn't such a far-fetched idea (though Fawcett would have been pushing eighty by then). In *Mysteries of Ancient South America* (1947), Wilkins wrote: "The Matto Grosso swamps and jungles are such queer places, with records of white men detained by Indian tribes for twenty-five or thirty years and then returning to civilisation, that one would not deem it impossible, if improbable, that Colonel Fawcett himself is still alive." Thus, searches continued. Even if there was little hope of recovering the members of the lost party, the mystery and adventure surrounding the chase offered the same pull to other adventurers as it did in the first place to Fawcett. Besides, snatches of news concerning Fawcett continued to leak out of the jungle for decades.

In 1950, the chief of the tribe that many presumed had killed the Fawcett party made a deathbed confession that he had murdered the three men because both Percy and Jack Fawcett had slept with his wife and because Fawcett had publicly humiliated him by slapping him. The confession was made to Orlando Vilas Boas of the Central Brazil Foundation. The chief, Izarari of the Kalapalos, passed his leadership on to a tribesman named Comatzi upon his death. Comatzi then instructed one of his tribesmen to take members of Boas's search party to a small gravesite and dig up Fawcett's bones; Rimell and the younger Fawcett, according to the story, had been thrown in the river. A major problem with this account: Fawcett was famously respectful to Indian tribes; the notion of his doing either of the two alleged acts was hard to believe. Brian Fawcett, Percy's surviving son, said it best when he wrote, "A man so utterly opposed to violence towards the Indians as to allow himself and his party to be shot at with poisoned arrows for a considerable time, and refuse to retaliate, is not the one deliberately to offer a mortal insult to a chief!" Ultimately, the recovered bones, sent back to England for analysis, proved to belong to someone else. The mystery endured.

In the three decades after his disappearance, at least a half dozen other Fawcett sightings were claimed. In various tellings, Fawcett was living as confused, ragged, married against his will to a tribal woman, or enjoying godlike status. In every case, none of the claims could be proved. And the Fawcett legend grew.

In the years immediately following his disappearance, a series of books about Fawcett appeared: *Man Hunting in the Jungle: Being the Story of a Search for Three Explorers Lost in the Brazilian Wilds,* by George Dyott (the North American Newspaper Alliance's searcher); *Brazilian Adventure,* by Peter

Fleming; and *Wilderness of Fools: An Account of the Adventures in Search of Lieut.-Colonel P. H. Fawcett,* by Robert Churchward. And of course, Brian Fawcett's *Lost Trails, Lost Cities* (published in America as *Exploration Fawcett*). These reignited, or maintained, interest in the missing explorer. Thereafter, Fawcett lapsed into semiobscurity, at least in North America. But in recent years, his name and his legend have re-emerged.

In 1996, James Lynch and René Delmotte set out looking for some answers to the Fawcett mystery and wound up instead lucky just to escape with their lives. Kalapalo Indians, the oft-alleged Fawcett killers, captured the duo and let them leave only after commandeering their equipment, some thirty thousand dollars' worth of film and television gear. Two years later, English explorer Benedict Allen followed in Fawcett's footsteps, recording his voyage with a video camera. A BBC special, *The Bones of Colonel Fawcett,* about Allen's search, aired the following year. Allen found a Kalapalo Indian who had been alive when Fawcett and his party had passed through. According to the Indian, Fawcett had camped close by and then set off farther into the jungle. All any of the tribe saw of him afterward were clouds of smoke coming from the forest five days later. The Indians followed the smoke but found nothing.

As evidence both of Fawcett's enduring popularity and the even more enduring difficulties in traveling to this part of the world, there have been more than a dozen search expeditions. And since Fawcett's disappearance more than eighty years ago, more than one hundred people have died while searching for him.

In 2004, a play about Fawcett by the Czech-born writer-director Misha Williams ran in London. *AmaZonia* purports to tell the "truth" about the Fawcett legend. According to Williams, *Exploration Fawcett* was merely a "smokescreen" foisted on the public by Brian Fawcett to keep his father's name unsoiled. The real reason Fawcett went into the jungle, Williams claimed, was to set up a cult that worshipped some type of she-god or spirit guide. The cult's central tenets revolved around theosophy, a philosophical thought system based on an understanding of nature through mystical insight.

Two times, in 1952 and 1955, Brian Fawcett led searches for his father, his brother, and Raleigh Rimell. He reported his findings in the book *Ruins in the Sky* (1957). He met with Kalapalo Indians but didn't find any conclusive evidence about the lost party.

It goes without saying that the young Brian would have been fascinated by his father's stories about the hidden world deep in the Brazilian jungle. And because of his father's well-earned prominence in exploration circles—a reputation stretching back to Brian's grandfather—the young Brian also had every reason to believe the claims. After all, his father, a very learned man, insisted on their veracity. In describing Z, Percy Fawcett wrote, "[It] is in a valley surmounted by lofty mountains. The valley is about ten miles wide, and the city is on an eminence in the middle of it, approached by a barrelled roadway of stone. The houses are low and windowless, and there is a pyramidal temple."

As Brian Fawcett and his team hacked through the difficult terrain on the second search, literally and figuratively following in his father's footsteps some three decades after the elder Fawcett's disappearance, Brian cleared a ridge and came upon the fabled city. "Yes, it was all here, exactly as described—from the strategically placed forts by the river to the pectinated summits of the cliffs, it was all here . . ."

Had Z actually been discovered? Had the son made it to the place the father had failed to reach? Were Fawcett's fantastical tales about to be proved true? Sadly, no.

Brian continues, "Our vantage point showed us clearly enough that man had no part in its making." Alas, Z was the work of nature, not human beings: "We had seen clearly enough how the thin top soil had gradually fallen away to disclose a belt of conglomerate, and we had seen the progressive erosion of this until it culminated in the seven pseudo 'cities.' The formation, probably deltaic, incorporated those convincing courses of masonry; wind and rain had slowly carved them up into the semblance of manmade edifices. *Sete Cidades,* the city linking Brazil with Atlantis, was an illusion. My father had believed implicitly in its genuineness, and I wondered if he would have pursued his quest to his undoing had he visited it before the fatal expedition."

Brian Fawcett held his father in great esteem and would have every reason, in compiling his father's writings, to support his great assertions. But having actually followed his steps, Brian reported that the city as his father envisioned it—at least in the place he had envisioned it—simply wasn't there.

The feeling of disappointment and sadness must have been overwhelming, tempered only by the passage of many years and the realization that though his final quest had been marked by a futile—and fatal—effort, Percy Fawcett left a legacy of exploration matched by few people over the course of the twentieth century. Brian wrote, "Had so many years not passed since my father's disappearance I might have felt more bitter than I did about the futility of his fate and that of the others—three lives lost or ruined in the quest for an objective that never existed . . ." It was a poignant and final rebuttal to his father's insistence.

But Percy Harrison Fawcett deserves that history treat him as the great adventurer and explorer he was, a man who did difficult and important work in some of the world's most inhospitable places.

Sadly, however, regarding what would have been his greatest historical coup, it turns out that he was, as far as we know in the present day at least, wrong. But who knows what future discoveries might bear him out? "Whether we get through, and emerge again, or leave our bones to rot in there, one thing's certain," he wrote. "The answer to the enigma of Ancient South America—and perhaps of the prehistoric world—may be found when those old cities are located and opened up to scientific research.

"That the cities exist, I know."

3/ The Honeymooners: Glen and Bessie Hyde

Drowning in a raging river is one of the worst ways to die, no doubt.

At first, however, it's not altogether different from jumping off the high dive. There's the initial crash and the pounding on the eardrums. Then comes an eerie quiet, a calm, before you break the surface, free to swim toward some friendly ladder, where you can do it all again. But after falling into the churning of a great river, after that initial thunderous roar, there comes a maelstrom of froth, currents, and kinetic strength so beyond your capabilities that you're at best a rag doll. You tumble over and over, watching—if you manage to keep your eyes open—as the swath of colors enveloping you goes from the benevolent opaque gray of near surface, to darker green or brown, to black. Here, in the blackness, the calm returns. Perhaps you have reached a pool where you can emerge, bloodied but unbowed, armed now with a greater sense of reverence and a great tale to tell friends around a campfire. But maybe there's something worse afoot here; maybe if you pushed toward the surface now, you'd find that you were merely headed deeper, and now you are tumbling some more.

You want to breathe; everything in your physiology tells you to. But you aren't panicked enough to forget that you can't breathe here. You have to wait, but that teasing lightness you saw when you first went under has long since disappeared. Now it's only blackness, maybe a flash of mocking emerald here and there.

But it's getting too difficult. The pressure to breathe is too great—literally. The carbon dioxide is building up in the lungs, and it needs to come out. And so what kills you under water, ironically, is the need to *exhale*. Once that's done, inhalation, of course, is right behind it.

Glen Hyde, a man of rugged good looks, tall and lean with a crescent of dark hair forever swooping over his forehead, was an individualist raised in even more rugged Idaho in the early part of the twentieth century. It was in Idaho where Glen met a boatman named Henry Guleke. Guleke introduced him to a boat called a scow, which is essentially a gigantic wooden box. It has no propulsion sans the river and is steered by two massive "sweeps," large oars in the front and back of the boat; for this reason, a scow was often referred to as a "sweepboat." It's a clunky-looking thing, seemingly ill suited for serious white-water navigation. But despite its unwieldy looks, it's actually quite maneuverable, and it proved to be a reliable vessel for northwest river trips.

Glen Hyde had done sweeps down the Snake River, which coils along the Oregon-Idaho border. He learned to love the scow and became very comfortable steering one, something accomplished without the psychological and physical security of a life jacket, which was rarely worn in those days, and never by Idaho boatmen. River running intrigued Hyde; he dreamt of running the length of the mighty Salmon River, which remains a beast to this day: dubbed the "River of No Return," it is the longest undammed river in the contiguous United States. Eventually, he would run the river with his sister Jeanne. It was a precursor to a fateful trip he would make with his future bride, a woman he did not yet know.

Bessie Haley was a bohemian, a spunky girl with a flapper hairdo. Her petite size (less than one hundred pounds) belied a steely strength that women in her day and age were not supposed to have. Especially ones who looked like Bessie, a very attractive, dark-eyed and dark-haired woman with an infectious smile. She studied art at Marshall College in West Virginia and in 1926 headed west to pursue art and poetry, eventually winding up in San Francisco at the California School of Fine Arts. And this intrepid young lady's travels didn't stop once she reached San Francisco. On a steamer from San Francisco to Los Angeles, accompanying a wannabe Hollywood starlet, Bessie Haley danced the night away and wound up meeting a man she would soon marry: Glen Hyde.

Colorado River

Their wedding in 1928 found the young couple in the midst of an exciting time, after World War I but before the Depression and World War II. It was the era of the barnstorming aviators, aerial entertainers who thrilled the country. Wing-walkers and the like suffused the end of the decade with a carefree attitude. They dressed in fancy costumes and performed acrobatics thousands of feet in the air, sometimes transferring from one plane to another midflight. People were busy throwing off the social shackles of the Victorian era. Folks blatantly flouted racial segregation, very much the prevailing societal and legal code, in clubs where women smoked cigarettes and danced on tabletops to Benny Goodman and Chick Webb. The country sat on the cusp of the great stock market crash that would send the nation into Depression, but for now, men (and women such as Bessie Hyde) could do wild and outlandish things.

It was time to renew Glenn's simmering dream of river running.

By 1927, grand expeditionary river runs had come into vogue; they rarely failed to garner great fame for the runners. Expeditions ran down the Green River in Utah and the Colorado in Arizona. The adventurous, newly married Hydes weren't immune to the national news and fervor over the daring voyages. These undertakings were no less than man's symbolic taming of the American

West, a place deeply entrenched in the imaginations, and still out of reach, of most Americans.

The Hydes planned to navigate more than six hundred miles of the Green and Colorado rivers, through the Grand Canyon, in seven weeks. They would make the trip in their homemade scow. If successful, the couple would go into the history books by completing the trip in so short a time. In fact, the Hydes set their sights on three records. They would also be the first people to run all the rapids in the river. Previous expeditions had portaged over many of the tougher rapids. In addition, Bessie would become the first woman to complete the feat. And she was the perfect candidate: sass and bravado all the way. In an era where divorce was relatively uncommon and many people looked down on a divorced woman as something of a strumpet, Bessie had married Glen the day after her divorce from her first husband became final. After a record-setting performance on the river, the two would be famous, and their immediate lives would be neatly mapped out for them: books, public appearances, speaking tours, movies.

The couple set out in October of 1928.

From a rim of the Grand Canyon, the Colorado River is merely beautiful, a shimmering ribbon of water snaking through the more imposing walls that hem it in. From above, where the rim in places is nearly a mile above the river's surface, the Colorado looks peaceful, serene, even tamed.

But once you're on the river itself, tugged along by its relentless force, the serenity imagined from above shatters into white foam, which slams the rocks littering its course.

Before the Hydes could get through the Grand Canyon, they had to get to it. Setting off from the small railroad town of Green River, Utah, they snaked along the Green River through Labyrinth Canyon and Stillwater Canyon. These are relatively straightforward runs, and, accordingly, the couple had an easy time of it. It took only a week before they reached the confluence of the Green and Colorado rivers. They were on their way.

But entering the Colorado from the Green drops one into Cataract Canyon, a difficult stretch of rapid-filled river that often takes boaters by surprise. The Hydes knew it was coming, but perhaps were not prepared for its force. Soon after entering Cataract, Bessie, easily twenty pounds lighter than the rear sweep, flew right out of the boat. Fortunately, Glen saw it coming, grabbed her ankle, and reeled her in before the river took her. The accident didn't leave them questioning the sanity of their mission, and ultimately, they would recount the story with jocularity. However, it couldn't have failed to shake them. Somewhere deep within, it must have lodged as a potential harbinger. The Hydes rollicked for two more days in Cataract, with its many rapids that had claimed a multitude of boats. But they made it. A few days removed from Bessie's scare, the couple easily regained the confidence and boldness that defined them.

The river towed them through Glen Canyon and Marble Canyon before they reached the granddaddy of them all: the Grand Canyon. At least initially, Glen wasn't overly impressed by the Grand Canyon. After successful runs down the Green and through the Cataract, he wrote: "The Grand Canyon is sort of disappointing after what we have seen. It is no grander than any of the other canyons we have come thru." A comparison of the jaw-dropping factor between the two rivers and their attendant canyons depends, of course, on the individual; however, if Glen Hyde felt that the relative lack of splendor in the Grand Canyon would be accompanied by a corresponding placidity in the river, he was dead wrong. But for now, they were doing what they set out to do—and having the time of their lives.

Bessie kept a journal, and it suggests an upbeat party, shaken here and there by large rapids, ill weather, and being knocked into the river. Both Glen and Bessie wrote of being thrown out of the boat, accounts retold to people they met along the way. But in all, the trip was a grand adventure, and the young woman and her new husband were having quite an escapade. In fact, nothing in Bessie's journal indicates that she found it too tough or that she wanted to quit. Additionally, some members of the press began to show up as the Hydes made their way down the Colorado River and well into the Grand Canyon. It was no flock of paparazzi, but word of the Hydes' attempt was starting to trickle out (at least locally).

As they make their way along the river, their faces fix in determined gazes as confident smiles simmer just below the surface. Glen mans the front oar while Bessie takes the rear. They float along at a steady pace, marveling at the scenery around them: puffs of green vegetation interspersed with a brown landscape. But this isn't simply "brown." The endless shades of brown outrun the imagination: sand, auburn, russet, tawny, coffee, each appearing and disappearing at the whim of the sun and clouds. Each etch in the wall contains a slightly different shade, a barely discernible variation on the same theme: it is monotonous only in its continuing beauty.

Some limestone and sandstone walls rise straight from the river, while others lend the weary traveler a beach to rest on. Built up from rockfall that traps the river's tremendous silt burden, they provide places for Glen to land the scow and scout upcoming rapids. On such sandy banks, Glen and Bessie tie their boat, make camp, eat next to a campfire, and lie on their backs, staring into a limitless sky punctuated by inestimable points of light. Here they feel their own insignificance, their immeasurable smallness in the great thrust of the universe. But in this infinitesimality, they see their grander purpose. Running this river, making the journey to its end—they will strike a blow against the anonymous toil that defines the vast majority of human lives. Here they will become legends.

Glen and Bessie fall into a routine. In the morning break camp. Then back on the boat. Enjoy the scenery and the thrill of doing this wonderful thing together. Negotiate and survive the rapids in due course.

After setting camp and hiking the Bright Angel Trail out of the canyon, Glen and Bessie met with well-known photographer Emory Kolb at his home on the rim. Kolb took a picture of the handsome couple on November 16, 1928. Glen is a good-looking man; his swoop of hair, large belt buckle, and pants cinched at the knees make him look like a stylish fellow of the 1920s or 1930s. But Bessie, somehow, looks thoroughly modern, as if the picture could have been taken yesterday. She wears a leather jacket with a fur-lined collar; her arms are tucked casually into the front pockets. It's a black-and-white photo, of course, but one can almost perceive the color in Bessie's dark eyes, sparkling and measuring the worth of her photographer. Life, a lack of fear, crackles just below the surface. In what was a popular compliment in its day, Bessie's brother had declared that "Bessie should have been a man."

However, several eyewitnesses to the trip suggested that Bessie was dejected and ready to give it up. In fact, a photograph taken two days after Kolb's by a tourist who ran some of the river with them shows that something had changed with Glen and Bessie. The couple wear the same clothing, but a slight downward cast to Bessie's eyebrows tempers the light that had emanated from her eyes. A smooth palate of skin above her nose in the first picture now is etched with two worried grooves. This time, only one hand sits within a pocket of her leather jacket. The other tightly clutches her hat, the veins and weatherworn knuckles looking as if they belong to a much older woman. Glen, too, looks older. His lips are pursed, and shadows paint the undersides of his cheekbones. Had something happened in between? Did they have an argument that dealt a fatal blow to their enthusiasm? Had they been thrown from the river again and received a serious scare? Or were they simply exhausted? Whatever the case, Bessie made no mention of it in her journal. To the end, she recorded no indication of anything terribly wrong aside from the difficulties one would expect from running such a river.

Something going wrong or scaring them terribly is all speculation anyway. We've all been victims of unflattering photographs, after all. But this image stands out, being virtually the only picture of the couple that exists in which they look plainly unhappy. It must be remembered that in this era before the heyday of the candid, unexpected photograph, people usually posed for their pictures. In this photograph, their last, neither Glen nor Bessie makes any attempt to hide whatever is eating at them. But back in the boat they went anyway, soldiering on whether their foul mood was merely a temporary blip or indeed an indication of something very wrong.

Years before the Hydes made their attempt on the Colorado River, the U.S. Geological Survey mapped out mileage markers, marking Lees Ferry, Arizona, as Mile 0. North Canyon sits at Mile 20, and then come the Roaring Twenties, a very tough stretch filled with monster rapids. Here, the couple noted much difficulty, from the boat being slammed against rocks to Glen being slammed in the face by his sweep. But in their journals and letters, the space they devote to their enthusiasm for the adventure and the majestic country surrounding them is at least equal to that dedicated to describing the problems: shrieking winds, pouring rain, snowstorms. Several references to abandoning the trip are recounted only with jest.

After making it through the difficult twenties and just beyond, Glen figured they were halfway through their journey and three weeks from completion. Anything going awry from there on could be tempered with the pronouncement that they'd already completed more than what lay ahead of them. *Just keep going.*

Plus, more press stories began to leak out. One in the *Denver Post* quoted Bessie as saying, "Our main object in taking this trip is to give me a thrill. It's surely been successful so far; I have had the thrills of my life and I've been thoroughly drenched a dozen times; but I am enjoying every minute of the adventure."

After their final meetings with witnesses to their trip—Kolb and the tourist who took the "unhappy photograph"—the Hydes were never seen nor heard from again. After two and a half weeks elapsed and Glen's father, Rollin, missed receiving an expected note from Glen telling of the couple's success and encampment in California, he set out immediately, fearing that something terrible had happened.

According to Bessie's journal, the Hydes made their final camp at Mile 210 and crossed their final rapid at Mile 217. Search parties would find Glen's tracks at virtually every major rapid; it was clear that as the couple approached a rapid, Glen would hop out of the boat, walk along the river, and scout the best route through. Although his tracks were found at 217, there was no sign of him (or Bessie) otherwise.

Bessie records Rapid 217, then a bit more river, and then her journal ends. If her final entry chronicles the last day of their voyage, the couple bested the river for forty-two days; the boat was found three weeks later.

The number of searches financed and spearheaded by Glen's distraught father reached the double digits over two and a half years, plunging him into poverty. It wasn't just grief or a refusal to accept the terrible truth that pushed the elder Hyde to continue. Any single search was invariably insufficient. The area was too untamed and remote, with millions of nooks capable of hiding a body or two. It was certainly possible to walk right by a corpse and not know it.

An air search located the scow at Mile 237, empty, upright, and full of the Hydes' possessions. In the two weeks after their disappearance and during subsequent failed search missions, the two became national news. But, as happens today, the press quickly moved on to the next sensational story once the couple were presumed dead.

Most agree that it was at Mile 232 Rapid where Glen and Bessie met their fate—it's a difficult rapid to maneuver and an even harder one to scout, offering precipitous rock and little in the way of beach. It also sits just beyond a bend in the river, shielding the rapid from view until one is right on top of it. There's little to no time to prepare. It is true that the Hydes devoured everything written about the river by the time of their trip. But nothing had been written by anyone who had attempted the river in a scow, which was really popular only in Idaho and waters farther north.

One can imagine the couple upriver as they approach 232, battling with their sweeps as they had in every other rapid. Their faces are full of resolve; they've come far, and there's no way they're quitting now. Bessie puts all of her ninety pounds into the back sweep, holding on with calloused hands, her sleek arms taut and sinewy. Glen bites hard on his pipe; he works the front sweep, pulling and pushing as the water froths and roars.

Then a moment of relaxation arrives. The water smooths. Hands remain on the sweeps, resting as much as they steer. The couple approach a curve and take the bend; there's a great thunder of water. It increases in intensity, and Glen tries to maneuver the boat to the side. But there's no landing area. Rocks rise from the river. Serrated boulders front the walls. Gusts of wind sweep through the canyon walls and threaten to send the boat crashing against the rocks. The onward-rushing, hell-bent river fights them, leading them toward boulders. Glen and Bessie work in tandem, in a well-orchestrated dance, keeping the boat precisely where they want it. And now they must head left, away from the saw-toothed rocks along the right side but away also from any safe place to stop and scout.

They rush toward the monster rapid. Glen attempts to push away from it; perhaps he can pin the boat in the calmer section of the river. Even if he can't get out and scout, if he can suspend the boat just upriver of this beast, he can plot his course through it. But it's too late. The wind shrieks; the water grabs and pulls them. The descent is swift and all-encompassing. Deafening pops and bangs engulf them; water spouts in every direction. Bessie loses sight of Glen as the boat charges into the rapid, drops precipitously, bounces on the surface, turns around, roils, bucks, pulls, and pushes. If only they could reach out to each other, grab hands, go down together.

The boat, in the end, survives, full of water but intact. But what of the honeymooners? Did they drown? Seems logical. They attempted to run a mighty river without life jackets, after all.

However, drowning has an almost unavoidable consequence: a body, no less two bodies, is virtually bound to turn up sooner or later. Even if both Glen and Bessie were pinned under some large object, surely seventy-plus years of current would have loosed at least one of them; surely some remnant would have emerged somewhere.

Besides, simple drowning doesn't speak to the imagination. A popular theory maintains that the couple ditched the boat somewhere near Mile 225, setting it adrift with their possessions inside, and hiked out of the canyon to start new lives elsewhere under new names and new identities. This is a romantic notion, but it doesn't add up. If they had undertaken this adventure in part to gain fame, why abandon it, and why abandon it so late in the game, when they had already accomplished so much? Plus, from what exactly would they have been running? Both had loving families, and both received much in the way of support in their quest. Why put loved ones through such grief, especially when those loved ones offered nothing but encouragement in return?

Whatever the case, all of Rollin Hyde's earnest attempts at finding them yielded nothing. The story of Glen and Bessie Hyde faded from prominence, living on only in the hearts and imaginations of those who loved them.

But all that would change some forty-three years after their disappearance.

During a river-running expedition in 1971, a woman named Elizabeth Cutler claimed to be Bessie Hyde. Cutler certainly seemed to be the right age. Some in her group dismissed it as a fireside prank, but the legend grew. It eventually became typical day's-end lore among river runners in the Grand Canyon, and it endured for almost twenty years.

According to "Bessie," she and Glen had had a big fight, and he roughed her up. (This could explain the sullen expressions on the pair's faces in their last photograph.) So, late at night, she stabbed him, sank the body, and let the boat go downstream. She hiked out of the canyon, "caught a Greyhound bus, and went back east."

Adding to the story is the strange fact that when Emory Kolb died in 1976, a skeleton was found in his boathouse. It had a bullet hole in the skull. This was another piece of the puzzle: Cutler ("Bessie") had hiked out but didn't dispatch her husband as claimed; either Emory Kolb or his brother Ellsworth killed Glen, and Cutler said she stabbed him to cover for Kolb. The motivation was clear: Glen was a grade-A jerk, and he needed to be disposed of. One of the Kolbs, who knew the couple well, did the deed because it was the manly thing to do. After all, they weren't immune to Bessie's persuasive charm. The story has holes, to be sure (if nothing else, why would a woman admit to a murder and expect no repercussion?), but that didn't stop its repetition and alteration after repeated retellings.

What isn't under dispute, and what would no doubt be at least a curiosity, if not a sight of homage, is an inscription at Narrow Canyon, just below Cataract Canyon: "HYDE 11-1-28." But even this one morsel (which would do nothing toward solving the mystery of the couple) has disappeared from view. Lake Powell has swallowed the floors and slots and with them, the inscription. Other evidence of the Hydes—a note, a torn shirt, bones, clothing remnants—have never been found, and so the legend has grown. Cutler's claim only enhanced it.

However, there are a few problems with Cutler's story and the skeleton in the Kolb boathouse. Multiple tests done on the skeleton concluded it was not Glen's body. Forensics experts determined the age of the skeleton at the time of death to be eighteen to twenty-two, a decade younger than Glen. Furthermore, those same experts declared that the skeleton predated 1920, eliminating the possibility that it was Glen Hyde.

Additionally, by 1990 Cutler's story had been thoroughly debunked by a curious investigative reporter. The fact that it persisted that long is astounding. A rudimentary investigation would have dispelled it easily. If nothing else, Cutler was almost a half foot taller than the diminutive Bessie. But in cases such as the Hydes', the legend is, somehow, larger than the person.

The mystery of their disappearance would get one more resurrection. When the immensely secretive but well-known river runner Georgie Clark died in 1992, it was learned, to everyone's astonishment, that Georgie Clark was really named Bessie DeRoos. Also, stories she'd told during her life—about living in Chicago, for example—turned out to be completely untrue. And most strangely, among her possessions was the marriage certificate of Glen and Bessie Hyde.

The speculation: Georgie (perhaps the real Bessie) had in fact killed Glen and subsequently made her living ferrying paying passengers down the river in a boat that was strikingly similar to the Hydes' scow.

Alas, this myth too breaks down. It's still a mystery why Georgie had the marriage certificate, but it was definitely a copy. It's also unclear why she made up so much of her biography, but research made it clear Georgie and Bessie were not the same person. Again, if nothing else, it's an issue of height: Georgie was a full five inches taller than Bessie.

But what of the fact that no sign of either body was ever found? There's an answer to that, too. The Colorado is thickly silted. Heavy sediment finds it way into the clothing of people washing down the river. All that extra weight quickly drags the person down to the bottom. As a result, in the early days of Colorado River exploration, drowning victims were rarely found.

The Hydes' story endures for some obvious reasons: it involves attractive people disappearing into the ether while undertaking something that the vast majority of human beings wouldn't do—or, at least, would never give themselves an opportunity to do. In the end, their story forces us to ask ourselves if *we* would be so daring. And for those few who answer yes, how many count themselves lucky enough to have found a mate who would heartily go along?

We are left to ponder the possibilities. Did they actually manage to "escape" their lives and live completely new ones, with new identities and new goals? Did they use a dangerous boat trip only as an opportunity for that "escape"?

Again, these things are unlikely, as the Hydes had more to gain from successfully completing the trip than abandoning it. However, it remains an attractive thought because there are so few among us who have never harbored at least a fleeting fantasy to chuck everything and go elsewhere. To do it with the one you love is even better.

The mystery of the Hydes' disappearance lasts because they are representative of the very river they tried to tame—bold, feral, full of risk and adventure. Visitors to the Grand Canyon know very well that a hundred trails and rim platforms and organized river trips couldn't even begin to tame the landscape, which will always be representative of America itself: free, wild, and forever in flux even as it seems immovable.

The Hydes, then, are the human embodiment of that notion: full of big ideas, possessing the gumption to put them into action, and then disappearing without a trace in the very land that best holds secrets. One must spend a lifetime to truly penetrate the wonder that is the American Southwest; perhaps, now into eternity, the Hydes have finally achieved it—as they themselves have become part of that landscape.

4 / The Deep Peace of the Wild: Everett Ruess

"It is not for us to play highway robber and hold up life . . . I doubt if death fulfills. It seems to end but I doubt it ends much. Not one's influence or the influence of one's work. Perhaps even the echoes of your voice may go on forever. Some instrument might pick them up years or ages hence."

—Christopher Ruess, in a letter to his son, December 10, 1933

"To die in the open, under the sky, far from the insolent interference of leech and priest, before this desert vastness opening like a window onto eternity—that surely was an overwhelming stroke of rare good luck."

—Edward Abbey

None of us has escaped the sickening sensation of falling from a dizzying height in a dream. We wake in a terrible panic, unable for a moment to catch our breath and bathed in a cool layer of sweat.

The sensations that accompany falling are universal. There will be an immediate springing of the limbs to try to hold something, the arms and fingers will grasp, the legs will shoot out, the torso will tighten in the anticipated shock of landing. It's one of the earliest tests a pediatrician performs on an infant: sit her upright and let her fall to the side (catching her before she hits, of course). Sure enough, without conscious signal, a healthy infant will project her hands to arrest her fall.

But what if we are adults, and it happens not as some test? If we have survived the deep fall, we may be left staring up at that place where we've just been. The physical perspective, obviously, has changed. But more than just that viewpoint has changed; there's shock now, and once that wears off, we might feel the excruciating crush of pain. Perhaps internal organs have been damaged; maybe they leak blood or bile or toxins. While we wait, the leakage is slowly poisoning us.

This is a terrible way to die, of course. But what if it happened in a place that we loved beyond measure? What if, in those last moments, the view we see from our backs is enough to fill us to the brim with ecstasy?

What if we allow a smile because we had been prophetic, had seen it all, had written a piece of fiction years earlier in which a lonely artist lay dying on the bottom of a canyon? His strength slowly disappears, yet "somehow, his happiness grew greater. He knew he could not get back, but he was content. All that was left of his anguish now passed, and a light shone in his eyes as he saw the dying sun flood the waste lands with splendor."

What if, then, we slowly succumbed, deciding that this was the very best way to go because, after all, it came on our terms and in a place we loved? This is what we can hope was the final fate of Everett Ruess.

On March 28, 1914, Everett Ruess (pronounced "ROO-ess") was born in Los Angeles into a family of influential people. Ruess's mother, Stella, was an accomplished poet and block printer, and an associate of several art and writing clubs. Stella even produced a journal, the *Ruess Quartette,* a creative outlet for the family's work. Her husband, Christopher, a graduate of Harvard Divinity School, was a deeply philosophical and intellectual man. Everett had an older brother, Waldo, who would work in no fewer than ten foreign countries and travel extensively in more than one hundred. It's interesting to note that some of Everett's early letters to Waldo suggest that he drop his sedentary life and choose adventure instead. Perhaps wanderlust was something inherent in the Ruess genes, or maybe the younger brother set an irresistible example for the elder.

Everett's eventual need to uproot may have begun early; by the time Everett was ready to enter high school, the Ruess family had moved from California all the way across the country to Brookline, Massachusetts, then halfway back—to Valparaiso, Indiana—before finally settling once again in Los Angeles. From there in the summer of just his seventeenth year, Everett took off, heading north up the Pacific Coast to Carmel and Big

Everett Ruess

Sur, and then Yosemite and the Sierra Nevadas. His parents encouraged him; his mother had similar freewheeling impulses, and his father saw this trip of self-discovery as a fine precursor to the "real life" of college and work that awaited him. His father had once written to him, "The thing for you to do is to stick to your hobbies, whether art, or naturalist's interest, or chemistry, and so know just what you are going to college for." Christopher Ruess hoped his son—whose intellect was clear from an early age—would eventually earn a degree. Everett showed little inclination toward that, however, opting instead to go where the road—or trail—led him. Nevertheless, Christopher Ruess did feel that his son's initial wanderings were "fully equal to any course at High School." Randall Henderson, an editor who compiled Ruess's writings in 1940, wrote, "Everett Ruess differed from others of his highly artistic temperament only in the fact that he had the opportunity and the courage and will to go forth and seek the realization of his dreams." This "opportunity" was the encouraging atmosphere in which Everett lived while at home.

The year 1930 saw the beginning of Everett's voluminous correspondence to friends and family from far-flung places. Indeed, an intriguing aspect of Everett Ruess's wandering is that it is narrated. Many decades later, we are the beneficiaries of what was private correspondence—including with himself. But what begins as private communication often turns out to be the truest reflection of people, and readers years hence are rewarded for being able to "eavesdrop" (think Anne Frank or Emily Dickinson). As with Anne Frank, it's easy to forget Everett Ruess's age when reading his correspondence. Almost all of his letters and diary entries were produced when he was only a teenager, beginning when he was sixteen. That's extraordinary, considering the lyricism and depth of thought contained within. For example, at sixteen, he described one of his camping spots along the Pacific this way: "The full moon illumined far-off whitecaps and the thundering cresters that shattered to spray in the tunnel, sending the expelled air past my face. Again, I heard the gull's spectral shriek, almost inaudible. I closed my eyes and slept."

His second letter home on that first trip in 1930 shows another singular characteristic of Everett Ruess: his unembarrassed habit of introducing himself to whoever he felt would provide him with a worthy intellectual or artistic experience. In a letter of June 30, Ruess wrote to his parents: "I went to Edward Weston's studio and made friends with him. A man who gave me a ride near Morro Bay had told me about him. I saw a large number of his photographs. He is a very broad-minded man." Edward Weston was (and is still today) widely considered one of this country's greatest photographers. He was also

almost thirty years older than Everett Ruess. But Ruess's bold introduction paid
dividends; the two hit it off, and Weston's simple but successful life as an artist—
relatively free of material possessions and knee-deep in art and beauty—would
serve as the model for which Ruess would, in his own way, strive.

Throughout that summer, Ruess continued to camp along the coast and
explore national parks. This early experience would prove to him two things:
the tug of the unknown was too much to resist, and he could navigate that
unknown successfully. Money and stability were mere encumbrances, other
people's conceptions of necessity. Not for the young Ruess; he had known it
before, but this trip confirmed it for him: his life would be different.

He returned home, finished high school in January 1931, and made plans
immediately to head to the wild and desolate Monument Valley on the Utah-
Arizona border. Monument Valley and Arizona's Painted Desert today can feel
like very lonely and isolated places; they were even more so in 1931, without
any paved roads and peopled almost entirely with Navajos unassimilated into
"European culture." For an impecunious teenager to head off into this area
alone was a move that was more than bold: it was harrowing.

But Everett reveled in it. His letters of that year burst with passion. On
April 18, to his friend Bill Jacobs, he wrote:

> *As for my own life, it is working out rather fortunately. These days
> away from the city have been the happiest of my life, I believe. It has
> all been a beautiful dream, sometimes tranquil, sometimes fantastic,
> and with enough pain and tragedy to make the delights possible by
> contrast. But the pain too has been unreal. The whole dream has
> been filled with warm and cool but perfect colors, and with aesthetic
> contemplation as I jogged behind my burro. A love for everyone
> and everything has welled up, finding no outlet except in my art.*
> [Ruess had taken up his mother's specialties: block printing and
> watercolors.]
>
> *Music has been in my heart all the time, and poetry in my
> thoughts. Alone on the open desert, I have made up songs of wild,
> poignant rejoicing and transcendent melancholy. The world has
> seemed more beautiful to me than ever before. I have loved the red
> rocks, the twisted trees, the red sand blowing in the wind, the slow,
> sunny clouds crossing the sky, the shafts of moonlight on my bed at
> night. I have seemed to be at one with the world. I have rejoiced to
> set out, to be going somewhere, and I have felt a sublimity, looking*

deep into the coals of my campfires, and seeing far beyond them. I have been happy in my work, and I have exulted in my play. I have really lived.

Also during this trip, Ruess undertook a strange habit, one that would color his disappearance three and a half years later. He altered his persona by changing his name. First, he became Lan Rameau. A letter of February 13 sent from Kayenta, Arizona, to his friend Bill ended with that French-sounding moniker. Also, he took to calling his burro Everett. All of this was a clever stab at self-deprecation. "Lan" is a bastardization of the French words for "the ass," *l'ane.* Thus, he was referring to himself as an ass and calling his ass Everett, "to remind me of the kind of person I used to be." A few weeks later, in a letter to his family, he asked, "Please respect my brush name . . . It's not the perfect cognomen, but I intend to stick by it." In a later letter to Bill, Ruess wrote of Lan Rameau, "the friend [unnamed] who helped me select it thought it was quite euphonic and distinctive." Nevertheless, the name didn't last too long. In a May 2 letter, Ruess wrote, "I have changed my name again, to Evert Rulan. Those who knew me formerly thought my name was freakish and an affectation of Frenchiness. It is not easy to choose a name, but Evert Rulan can be spelled, pronounced, remembered and is moderately distinctive. Of course, I changed the donkey's name. He is now definitely titled Pegasus."

Though the name-changing has a decidedly playful tone, there is in it an obvious psychological stab at rebirth. It seems that even the constant reinvention given him by the sun and colors and endless beauty of the American West that he loved so well weren't enough to soothe his need to constantly be born anew.

In fact, interspersed within all of Ruess's extolling of the beauty around him, the doubts about himself and his place within the larger world begin to creep in; these pessimistic tones would become part of a pattern that would remain for the rest of his short life. There are in these complaints hints of isolation the otherwise affable young man felt toward the rest of humanity. In May 1934, toward the end of his life, he would write, "Often I am tortured to think that what I do deeply feel must always remain, for the most, unshared, uncommunicated." Even earlier, there were suggestions of this lonely condition. In a May 2, 1931, letter to his brother, Waldo, Ruess wrote: "I must pack my short life full of interesting events and creative activity. Philosophy and aesthetic contemplation are not enough. I intend to do everything possible to reach the fullest development. Then, and before physical deterioration obtrudes,

I shall go on some last wilderness trip, to a place I have known and loved. I shall not return."

That last line is one that future conspiracists would pounce on to explain Ruess's disappearance, but more about that later. It's a bit puzzling that a young man of sixteen, at the height of his physical powers, should be worrying about "physical deterioration" and using the adjective "short" to describe his life when he is obviously projecting into the future with the verbs "must" and "intend."

It becomes clear that all is not well. A large part of the problem, as Ruess would reiterate in letters and diary entries for years to come, is his perceived inability to find, for lack of a better phrase, a "soul mate," someone who shared his particular outlook on the world. The problem is that said outlook included a healthy disdain for all those who didn't spend their lives in constant contemplation of beauty and art, and who didn't uproot themselves and forsake comfort to attain that life. Of course, that included the great majority of humanity. This conflict is summed up in the April 18, 1931, letter to Bill: "I have had many sublime experiences which the presence of another person might well have prevented, but there are others which the presence of a perceptive and appreciative friend might have made doubly worthwhile." And, in a letter dated August 27–28, sent from Zion National Park in Utah, he wrote to Bill:

> My friends have been few because I'm a freakish person and few share my interests. My solitary tramps have been made alone because I couldn't find anyone congenial—you know it's better to go alone than with a person one wearies of soon. I've done things alone chiefly because I never found people who cared about the things I've cared for enough to suffer the attendant hardships [Ruess had recently suffered an extreme case of poison ivy that left him hospitalized for eight days.] But a true companion halves the misery and doubles the joy.

Increasingly, Everett Ruess's main conflict comes into sharper relief: he is trapped by his insatiable desire to tramp the wilderness, which relegates him to being alone. However, it's clear that he desires the company of people, but only people who understand one's need to venture out alone in the same way. A May 29, 1932, diary entry: "I wish I had a companion, some one who was interested in me. I would like to be influenced, taken in hand by some one, but I don't think there is anyone in the world who knows enough to be able to advise me. I can't find my ideal anywhere." There are teases of this hoped-for companionship during his travels; Ruess often came across ranchers, travelers, and park rangers. One young man, Virgil, the son of a rancher for whom Ruess did a little work, presented himself as a potential kindred spirit. Ruess described him this way: "He is a pugilist but has appendicitis, and his girl made him promise to stop fighting anyway. He writes poetry of a sort. I showed him my stuff." But Virgil's father spent the next day trying to "save" Ruess from his lack of religious conviction, saying that "Science was leading [Ruess] to the devil." These interactions forced Ruess to set off again, disappointed. Ruess described himself as an "agnosticist," writing, "I don't see how an intelligent person can believe anything, even determinism . . . I can't believe in God just because other people do, and because they consider me good or wicked according as I believe or not."

There was also someone named Frances, a person Ruess described as "one girl with whom I am intimate." Ruess wrote several intense letters to her, but in the absence of both any further knowledge about who she was and her reply letters, it's unclear what caused the severance of their relationship or why Ruess found it more prudent to go back into the wilderness instead of returning to the city to be with her. (Perhaps doing otherwise would have been an impossibility; he hints at this in a July 12, 1932, diary entry: "God, how the wild calls to me. There can be no other life for me but that of the lone wilderness wanderer. I think I'll extend my leave another year. I'd get a couple of good horses and a good saddle. The wild has an irresistible fascination for me. After all, the lone trail is the best.") As for Frances, Ruess writes only, "I was sorry . . . that our intimacy, like many things that are and will be, had to die with a dying fall." A later letter hints that perhaps Frances had asked Ruess to come back and join her in the city, but that he told her he thought it impractical. His response to her letter begins, "I was surprised and pleased to receive your letter a couple of days ago. Glad too that you are getting something out of life. It shocked me slightly when you spoke of my greed for life. That is a harsh word, but I guess it is true. I am not willing to take anything but the most from life."

Despite Ruess's general misgivings about humanity, the young man certainly couldn't be called a misanthrope. Randolph Jenks and Tad Nichols years later told of the time they, as high schoolers, were traversing the Arizona desert in their pickup when they spotted Ruess on his donkey. Ruess was washed out, moving slowly, and slightly disoriented. The two men asked him if he wanted water; misunderstanding the question, Ruess reached for his own canteen, which was almost empty, and handed it to them. Nichols wrote a letter to *Desert Magazine* in 1939 as a follow-up to an April letter to the publication. He recalled being touched by the gesture: "He had very little water, but was immediately willing to share it with others."

By wintertime, Ruess hitchhiked back home to Los Angeles, waiting out the colder months until March 1932, when he headed back to the desert. It was clear that city life was merely a hiatus from the real life he enjoyed: the wild, desolate splendor of the American Southwest. But there was at least the implication of turning his wanderings into something that resembled a career, a thing that he abhorred but that fell in line, no doubt, with the aspirations of his college-age acquaintances back home. He would use the desert's landscapes to provide material for his art; just before coming back home to Los Angeles, he wrote: "My plan is to amble around the Southwest with donkeys for a couple of years more, gathering plenty of material and mastering watercolor technique—then to get some windfall so I can work with oils and do things on a larger scale, perfect my field studies, and then do something with what I have." However, as he noted, "I am not sure that I am an artist. I might try writing my adventures, but the personal element makes that very difficult. I could never endure any position with routine, regular hours, and monotonous work. Unless I am having new experiences, broadening horizons, some sort of change, I cannot feel life is worth living."

It would be ideal if his desert could be his meal ticket—but in the end this meant spiritually more than in any other sense. The desert was a place he simply couldn't let go. By the time of his disappearance, at age twenty, Ruess would spend large chunks of five successive years roaming the wilds: while this isn't such a terribly long period, it constitutes a quarter of the young man's entire life.

By mid-1932, as Reuss was tramping around the Navajo Reservation, the lure of the wild had only intensified. In a July letter to brother Waldo, Ruess wrote: "I have been thinking more and more that I shall always be a lone wanderer of the wilderness. God, how the trail lures me. You cannot comprehend its resistless fascination for me . . . I'll never stop wandering. And when the time comes to die, I'll find the wildest, loneliest, most desolate spot there is." While many of the areas he visited during this period have become accessible by asphalt and well-beaten tourist trails, in Ruess's time Shiprock, Mesa Verde, Canyon de Chelly, and the whole of Monument Valley were very remote places, full of Indian cliff dwellings that had not yet been excavated or protected. Indeed, Ruess would spend many nights in abandoned Indian hogans and days poking around ancient cliff dwellings, occasionally picking up pieces of jewelry and potsherds. In a diary entry of July 1932, Ruess hints at the ephemeral nature of his own existence, perhaps unwittingly, as he described a hogan he had returned to after camping there months earlier: "The babyboard was where I left it . . . except that the hoops had fallen into the bin. My printing on the board—Evert Rulan, etc.—was almost obscured. The rain washed away my tracks. The saddle is well cached. The ghosts of the cliff dwellers will guard it. I do not think I will return for it, however."

By autumn, Ruess returned home and to his father's relief, enrolled at UCLA. He didn't do entirely well; given the young man's intellect, the reasons had undoubtedly more to do with the strictures of formal education than the demands of the course work. In any case, after one semester, he was gone, planning a return trip to the wilds, this time the High Sierras of California.

There, he wrote of his UCLA experience to a friend named Bob: "How little you know me to think that I could still be in the University. How could a lofty, unconquerable soul like mine remain imprisoned in that academic backwater, wherein all but the most docile wallow in a hopeless slough?" Early in 1934, Everett wrote about college to his father: "I have tasted your cake, and I prefer your unbuttered bread. I don't wish to withdraw from life to college, and I have a notion, conceited or not, that I know what I want from life, and can act upon it." Here, and elsewhere, it's easy to see Everett Ruess as a sober and overly serious type. However, he had great capacity for humor; indeed, when people could get past his sometimes overbearing passion, they found him exceedingly good-natured. His diaries are peppered with witty lines such as, "A burro always has the gift of making you feel that you are a bigger ass than he is."

In October 1932, Ruess came out from the wild and headed back to the city: this time not to his home of Los Angeles, but to the more bohemian San Francisco. Here, Ruess would come smack up against his main conflict: the interminable pull of the untamed landscapes versus the desire for the companionship of compatible people that he could find only back in the cities. San Francisco would prove the best place for the latter. Here, he would strike up friendships with artists and intellectuals. True to his previous form, his method of introduction was simply arriving at these people's residences and studios and knocking on the door. As testament to his personality, he was met more often than not with welcome; periods of artistic and cultural immersion were sure to follow.

On October 24, 1933, in a letter to his family, Ruess mentioned his meeting with the accomplished painter Maynard Dixon and remarked, "I have liked his work for a long time, and the man himself is interesting." Dixon was almost sixty years old, but he received Ruess with enthusiasm, helping the younger man with his own artwork. According to Ruess, "The main thing Maynard did was to make me see what is meaningless in a picture, and have the strength to eliminate it; and see what was significant, and how to stress it." Coincidentally, Dixon had spent a lot of time in the desert Southwest, in the very same spots that Ruess had become so familiar with. Many of Dixon's paintings featured these very landscapes, and the two spent much time reminiscing about the places that they both loved.

What undoubtedly made Dixon even more appealing was the fact that, aside from being a talented painter, he was also married to the accomplished photographer Dorothea Lange, who would eventually earn fame for her Dust Bowl photographs of despondent migrants. Before that, however, she did a few photographic studies of Ruess that exist today as some of the most popular images of the young man. They are extraordinary in that they clearly capture the very haunting conflict that was Everett Ruess himself: the excruciating divide between man and boy. In one photo, Ruess's face emerges in bright light from the shadow of a large, black Stetson. A white, triangular collar rests against a dark sweater. The face is cast in bold, dark lines at the mouth, under the nose and eyebrows, and running from the cheek down to the Adam's apple. Absent from the face are chiseled lines or pocks that would suggest a life exploring out on the range or poking around high mountains or desert washes. It is a face, despite having been at the mercy of the elements for long periods, which still retains a youthful smoothness and an overall aura of optimism and possibility. Another photo, this one without the hat, reveals a wide, smooth forehead under thick hair, a good set of sturdy teeth, and a smile on Ruess's face that is unabashedly open and given to its photographer. Indeed, because of the age difference (Lange was nineteen years older than Ruess), he undoubtedly felt he was in the presence of someone much like his own artistically inclined mother.

Ruess had another reason for optimism; he was beginning to get established as an artist. He managed to get a series of his block prints up for consignment at the Paul Elder Bookstore, a famous spot for artists. It was, no doubt, a heady time. Ruess also notes in his letters that he busied himself with going to see films, operas with violinist Mischa Elman and by Rimsky-Korsakov, and speeches by singer, actor, and social activist Paul Robeson. A letter home, dated October 29, captures Ruess's exhilaration: "All's well, and I'm on the crest of the wave again as I hope you are, too. I have finally found myself, and have been busy painting all day. Yesterday I heard four symphonies, and then spent the afternoon and evening with Maynard Dixon, his wife Dorothea, and Ernst Bacon, a musician, and some other artists. I had a grand time, and it was certainly good to be among friends and artists again." Ruess also met up with a photographer who still commands wide name recognition today; in a follow-up letter home, he wrote, "Ansel Adams waxed very enthusiastic about my black and white work."

In spite of all this excitement in the city, and the usually overwhelming optimism that laces his letters, not all was perfect with Ruess. To his brother on December 22, he wrote, "Perhaps . . . it is just because I am nineteen and sensitive, but it is small consolation to be told that. I have been discovering new moods, new lows, new and disturbing variations in myself and my feelings for individuals, and people as a whole. On the other hand, there is a lot of fun in me yet, and I have had some unusually gay times that were not feverishly so. But for the most part there has been an undercurrent of resentment or unrest." Later, in the same letter: "After various turnings, twistings, and recoils, I still have not been able to find any proper outlet for my feelings. Perhaps there is none and perhaps it is necessary for my feelings to die of weariness and refusal." This sentiment mirrors earlier complaints. From a May 31, 1932, diary entry: "I [feel] distinctly different from other people; already I've drifted too far away from other people. I want to be different anyhow, I can't help being different, but I get no joy from it, and all the common joys are forbidden me."

In March 1934, Everett finally went back home. But he would only stay a month, time enough to plan the next trip: back to the Southwest, with northern Arizona and southern Utah his destination. It would be the last time Everett Ruess would ever be home.

Everett arrived in Escalante, Utah, an out-of-the-way Mormon town, during the second week of November 1934. His plan was to use Escalante as his base of operations for revisiting Zion and Bryce canyons, among other desert landscapes. During his short time in Escalante, he was something of a sensation. Not too many outsiders ever graced the town, and none like Everett Ruess. He was outgoing and, well, odd: he arrived on his burro, seemingly materializing from the waves of desert heat, his feet scraping the ground and his sacks full to overflowing. He spent his last night in town catching a movie with a ten-year-old named Norm Christensen. Then he was off, heading to the spectacular Davis Gulch canyon, through which the Escalante River flows. On November 11, from Escalante Rim, Everett Ruess wrote his last letter. It contains some lines that have become among the more famous to Ruess enthusiasts, including sentiments that led the Pulitzer Prize–winning writer and environmentalist Wallace Stegner to compare the young Ruess to the legendary conservationist and Sierra Club founder John Muir. Ruess's words: "As to when I shall visit civilization, it will not be soon, I think. I have not tired of the wilderness; rather I enjoy its beauty and the vagrant life I lead, more keenly all the time. I prefer the saddle to the streetcar and star-sprinkled sky to a roof, the obscure and difficult trail, leading into the unknown, to any paved highway, and the deep peace of the wild to the discontent bred by cities." He signed off, "It may be a month or two before I have a post office, for I am exploring southward to Colorado, where no one lives. So, I wish you happiness in California. Affectionately, Everett."

Escalante Rim, now part of the Glen Canyon National Recreation Area, is something of a nature lover's paradise—cliffs rising thousands of feet, snaky rivers, red rocks, slot canyons. Cottonwood trees and low-lying vegetation line the banks of the Escalante River. Natural arches wind away from canyon walls and then plunge deeply into shaded pools. Indian ruins line the canyons. It's a place that can overawe anyone, but for someone like Everett Ruess, the area was perfection. Ruess set up camp.

A week after writing his last letter, he came upon Addlin Lay and Clay Porter, two sheepherders camped nearby. He got their advice on nearby Indian dwellings and ruins. Ruess shared camp with the two men, politely refused their offer of mutton, and set out. No reliable reports of his sighting followed.

Because Ruess had advised his family that he would be away from a post office for months, there was little anxiety when they didn't hear from him. But when a stack of their unopened mail for Everett was returned to them in early February from Marble Canyon, Arizona, Stella and Christopher Ruess became alarmed. They wrote letters to the postmasters of several towns in northern Arizona and southern Utah, and by mid-February, the story of the missing artist from Los Angeles was getting national newspaper exposure. There was some reason to feel secure, however: most of the correspondence sent to the Ruesses coming from those who had met Everett assured them that the boy knew his way around the demands of the landscape and was very competent in this regard.

Still, a search party set out from the vicinity of Escalante and, on the advice of the two sheepherders who had shared camp with Ruess, quickly covered several area gulches. The search party concentrated mostly on Davis Gulch because it spotted Ruess's two loose burros eating grass nearby. A containing fence held a bridle and halter. But no Ruess.

As the group moved on, passing another arch, one of the searchers discovered four Anasazi pottery vessels and an intriguing find: the words "NEMO 1934" etched into the floor of the gulch. All around, they found Ruess's footprints as well as the detritus of a camp. Clearly, this is where he had stayed. But subsequent searches below the camp failed to turn up anything else.

Despite the failure to turn up a body, it's entirely conceivable that Ruess suffered a fall and was out of sight nearby. He had undertaken many dangerous moves before, and this was definitely the type of landscape that could hide a fallen body. It's also very important to note that the searches at Davis Gulch were done on horseback; failure to put feet on the ground and crawl into tight spots could easily mean the searchers literally walked right past, or above, Ruess's body. Then a flash flood could later do its work, and all traces would vanish. But even so, that would mean that Ruess had to have been holding all of his camping gear, for none of it was found. And because of the amount that he packed, he couldn't have carried it all out after setting his burros loose. An obvious rebuttal is that someone came along later and stole the camping equipment. It's a quick and easy leap then to the next idea, far more sinister: Everett Ruess was murdered, his body disposed of, and his possessions stolen.

But first, what of that cryptic carving, "NEMO 1934"? When asked, Ruess's father, Christopher, replied by telegram to a member of the search party: "Everett read in desert Greek poem Odyssey, translated by Lawrence of Arabian desert. Here Odysseus Greek word for nobody, 'Nemo' being Latin word for nobody. Odysseus trapped by man-eating giant in cave, saves own life by trick of calling himself Nemo. Everett dislikes writing own name in public places." There are certainly reflections of Everett in Odysseus's story. He wasn't averse to calling himself by a name other than his birth name; he had changed his moniker twice before. And there was little doubt that it was Ruess who had carved "NEMO." In fact, his shoe prints were later found in a different section of Davis Gulch next to another "NEMO 1934" carving.

There's another literary character aside from Odysseus that is perhaps more apt, one that eventually occurred to Christopher Ruess. Nemo is the name of the mysterious submarine captain in Jules Verne's fantastic *Twenty Thousand Leagues under the Sea,* a book with which Ruess was very familiar. Captain

Nemo forsakes all the laws of a barbaric human society and submerges himself into an aquatic world where he need not be bothered by the ferocity of human dealings. Could he have been Everett Ruess's model?

As for the theory of murder, many people believed it—including, eventually, Ruess's parents. The Escalante Rim area had seen a spate of cattle thievery just prior to Everett Ruess's appearance there. While a stray head gone missing here and there could be expected, even tolerated to a degree, local cattle owners apparently had had enough. They spread a false story that they had hired an agent who would be patrolling the area on the lookout for rustlers. Thus, any cattle rustlers would have viewed a stranger asking after the geography and cliff dwellings as a prime suspect. Would one of them be so disposed toward violence that he would kill the kid and dispose of the body?

Or perhaps it was someone else entirely. Some say a Navajo named Jack Crank—those who knew him agreed that his last name served as a representative description of his character, but multiplied a hundredfold—had murdered Ruess. One suggestion had it that he simply hated white men and that when he came across the lone boy, he killed him to soothe, at least temporarily, that seething odium. Another theory was that Crank needed the scalp of a white man for ceremonies. Indeed, later rumors spread across the Navajo Reservation that the scalp of a white man was being used in ceremonial dances; a bit of it was sliced off and used in subsequent dances, and then the entire thing was buried in an effort to exterminate its spirit. Even if these rumors were true, there is no evidence to suggest that the scalp was Ruess's.

Christopher and Stella came to believe that Crank was the killer of their son, based mostly on the fact that Crank, serving time in a Phoenix jail for an unrelated charge, boasted of having killed the boy and buried his body. Crank said he then took Ruess's burros miles away. If this was true, it would explain the distance between camp items found years later and the burros. However, it wouldn't explain why Ruess's footprints—and no one else's—and bedroll imprints were found at Davis Gulch, near the burros. Also, it turned out that Crank was an inveterate liar, and little of what he said could be believed.

Whether the killer was a cattle rustler or a homicidal Navajo, in the immediate aftermath of extensive searches, the verdict was murder. In August 1935, the *Salt Lake Tribune* sent investigative reporter John U. Terrell to hire a team, led by an Indian tracker named Dougeye, to see what had become of the young Ruess. The serialized articles, appearing under the tag, "S.L. Tribune Expedition into Desert Finds Clues to Fate of Young Artist," summed up the findings this way: "Everett Ruess, 21-year-old missing Los Angeles artist, probably met death at the hands of a renegade bad man or Indian in a lonely canyon near the southern end of the untracked Escalante desert. This is the united belief of the best Indian and white trackers, traders and wilderness residents of southern Utah and northern Arizona." The paper reached this theory partly because of what Ruess carried with him—saddle packs, Navajo blankets, silver and turquoise jewelry, a camera, cash, and "good outdoor clothing." This would have made him an attractive target for "either a red or white outlaw, and especially renegade wilderness Indians."

Another, more romantic, theory has taken hold since Ruess's disappearance. Carrying out his Nemo-esque desire to "break the ties of humankind," Ruess saddled up and entered the Navajo Reservation, where he married and lived his life among the Indians, never to return to the "civilization" he was born into and had grown incurably weary of.

In the 1930s, very few white people had any intimate contact with Native Americans in the desert Southwest. Those who did were primarily operators of trading posts, who saw profit as the main tie between themselves and the Indians. This state of affairs was due mostly to the Navajos' geographic isolation from American towns and cities, and it was exacerbated by the Indians' understandable distrust of white men. Everett Ruess was an exception to this rule. He got himself invited to a Hopi Antelope Dance, where he was the only white person. He also managed to ingratiate himself with influential Navajos. To his friend Bill in June 1934 he wrote:

> I have often stayed with the Navajos; I've known the best of them, and they were fine people. I have ridden with them on their horses, eaten with them, and even taken part in their ceremonies ["assisting and watching a Navajo sing for a sick woman"]. Many are the delightful encounters, and many the exchange of gifts I've had with them . . . Their weird, wild chanting as they ride the desert is often magnificent, with a high-pitched, penetrating quality . . . Beauty has always been my god; it has meant more than people to me. And how my god, or goddess, is flouted in this country, which to me is the most beautiful I've known in all my wanderings! It has come to the point where I no longer like to have anything to do with the white people here, except to get supplies and go on, and I think I shall not say any more what I do here.

Had Ruess simply had enough of the life he was born into? Despite his intoxicating few months in San Francisco, did he feel that a return there would offer nothing but new frustrations at his inability to adequately express through art and words the beauty and splendor of the natural world he loved so well?

The quixotic image of Ruess, perpetuated over the years by amateur investigators and distant admirers, is one of a lonely and frustrated boy who ran off because it was all he could do, forsaking all ties to the world he once knew. But those who were on the receiving end of his copious correspondence, though acknowledging the sometimes-desperate tone of his letters, knew better. Ruess's primary problem was that he desired company—but a specific type of company—so much that it frustrated him. To suggest he would give up at the age of twenty and call the search hopeless and futile is ignoring the fact that not long before his disappearance he had found that very companionship he desired so much back in San Francisco. His intent all along was to go back into the wild—he would probably never stop doing that so long as he drew breath—but to eventually return to a city to enjoy art and intellectual company. He had already had a taste of it, and enjoyed it immensely.

People can read certain passages in his letters and diaries and say that Everett Ruess did seem disposed toward suicide or planned disappearance, but he was someone who couldn't stop dreaming about the balance between blissful natural solitude and the companionship of someone he truly loved. He had hints and teases of the latter, and the former in abundance. It seems these would have been enough to keep him going. He also had dreams of art— painting, wood prints, poetry. It makes sense that he would have spent more time pursuing these. A July 25, 1932, diary entry: "While there is life, there is hope. I still think at times that the future may hold happiness. I shall wait and see. I have waited three years already, and not in vain. If for no other reason, I'll wait to hear more music. I never can hear enough." Some would argue that this was a solid two years before Ruess's disappearance, and, of course, much can happen and change in such a time, especially when that is more than a tenth of an impetuous young man's life. But this was also a year before his time in San Francisco, when he learned that the very things he did desire so much did exist and were available to him. In fact, in October 1933, he confided to his diary that his "heart sang at the anticipation" of getting to San Francisco, where he would live out his bohemian dreams.

The preponderance of letters more than suggest a need for constant connection to people, if not actually in person, then at least in spirit. To give all this up to go live with the Navajos doesn't jibe with his character. After all, though he admired the Navajos, they certainly didn't provide the type of intellectual stimulation—painting, opera, cinema, books—that he so craved. In his journals, kept during his sojourns in 1932 and 1933 (his 1934 journal has never been found), there are constant references to books; he was forever asking his family to send them. They became his steady companions, and he wasn't averse to literary criticism: "Finished the Brothers Karamazov. It fell flat toward the end, and I didn't like Dostoievsky's chatty way of speaking, but it was a real book." He would finish a series of books, send them home, and then request others. His book list in these years reads like a rigorous literature course's requirements in the Western Canon: among other authors and titles, Ruess read Thomas Mann's *The Magic Mountain;* the letters of Mendelssohn, Wagner, and Liszt; *The Arabian Nights;* "Rip Van Winkle"; *The Fifty Best Poems of America;* George Bernard Shaw's *Socialism for Millionaires; Through the Looking-Glass; The Story of Aristotle's Philosophy;* the essays of Ralph Waldo Emerson; Henrik Ibsen's *Ghosts;* Poe; Whitman; T. S. Eliot; Browning; Shakespeare; Yeats; Shelley; Wilde; Nietzsche; Rabelais; Omar Khayyám; Chekhov; Anatole France; *The Travels of Marco Polo.* He was very taken with the tales of *The Arabian Nights* as well as the *Rubaiyat.* He literally sang the latter book's praises, his vocal exuberance bouncing off the canyon walls and rock faces as he traveled the trail.

Also, this was a man who was very close to his family members. They made it possible for him to pursue his lonely wanderings, occasionally sending him money and supplies. It's illogical that he would have felt comfortable simply severing ties and letting them stew forever afterward with the pain of his disappearance. It must be remembered that Ruess hit upon something bordering fame only after he disappeared. Had he written his family and told them of his intention to "disappear" into Navajoland, no doubt they would have respected his wishes. At this point, after five years of wanderings, they certainly didn't hold out any hope that he would simply "get it out of his system" and come back home to settle down into a "respectable" position. Further, had he gone onto the Navajo Reservation to stay, no one would have come looking for him, save maybe a father or brother trying to persuade him to come back home, knowing all the while the futility of their attempt. This is confirmed by something his father wrote in 1940, six years after Everett's disappearance: "Even were he found alive, we would have no desire to interfere with his fulfillment of his life and destiny." Another fact argues against Ruess's having disappeared into the Navajo Reservation, this one offered by

Terrell of the *Salt Lake Tribune:* "A white youth who had come to live among [the Navajo] would be the choicest subject for gossip. The Indian would set out to learn why the white youth had come there to live; what were his intentions; why could he not dwell among his own people?" Ruess's living on the reservation incognito would require the complicity of every member of the tribe, something far-fetched indeed.

Perhaps the most logical explanation of the disappearance of Everett Ruess is that he simply fell to his death in the rugged and desolate terrain of the desert Southwest and that the landscape has held the secret and the body, shielding it from easy view and assuring its slow but complete absorption into the earth.

His letters describe many events that could presage the end of his life. From a July 15, 1932, diary entry: "With difficulty I climbed on a ledge and followed it till it shelved off and I was below the lower dwelling. For a long time I looked at the dwelling and shuddered. Once I made as if to climb up, but the rock crumbled. There was absolutely nothing to brace myself on. The cliff fell sheer away below." In this case, Ruess was prudent; he didn't attempt any further climbing. However, he would become more and more bold. On August 25, 1932, he wrote his family from Colorado of a narrow escape where he cheated death. Because he survived and because it was a great adventure, he tells it almost flippantly, as if relishing the humor in it. However, the experience does hint at the very real danger Ruess would put himself into. This danger would increase over the years, as he managed to survive one close call after another. He wrote:

> *This afternoon I returned from a four-day trip to Wild Horse Mesa and the North Escarpment. I visited several small cliff dwellings, some of them so situated as to be nearly inaccessible . . . There was one small dwelling which could only be reached by a ledge, from six inches to a foot and a half wide. Below was a sheer drop of fifty feet or so. I had little trouble entering it, being right-handed, but when it came to returning, matters were more complicated, I could not get by the narrow part with my back to the cliff, and if I faced the cliff, I had to go backwards and could not see where to set my foot. After three false starts, I finally reached level sandstone, by crawling on my knees. There was another dwelling near Horse Springs, which could only be reached by worming up a nearly vertical crevice, part of the way hanging by my hands. Even after that, I had to cross a wide creek and crawl under a boulder on the brink.*

On May 2, 1931, from Kayenta, Arizona, Ruess wrote: "Many times in the search for water holes and cliff dwellings, I trusted my life to crumbling sandstone and angles little short of the perpendicular, startling myself when I came out whole and on top." Another letter describes more disturbing experiences: "Day before yesterday I narrowly escaped being gored to death by a wild bull, and there was a harrowing sequel when he discovered my camp that night, somewhile between midnight and dawn. Yesterday I did some miraculous climbing on a nearly vertical cliff. One way or another, I have been flirting pretty heavily with Death, the old clown."

Ruess's descriptions of so many close calls were not merely youthful braggadocio. In July 1934, Ruess hooked up with some student archaeologists investigating Anasazi ruins in Utah and Arizona. Ruess signed onto the expedition, serving as cook, and used the spectacular beauty of the area as a staging ground for producing watercolors and block prints. Lead archaeologist H. C. "Clay" Lockett was consistently horrified at the chances Ruess took to get the best vantage point. In a letter to *Desert Magazine* in 1939, Lockett wrote, "One time in camp he stood on the edge of a 400-foot cliff in a rainstorm and did a water-color sketch of a waterfall . . . I personally was scared to death just watching him perched on the edge of the cliff." As to what happened to the young man, Lockett added, "It is my idea that some place while climbing the cliff . . . he may have possibly fallen to his death."

In a May 1934 letter to Frances, the girl with whom he had been involved in San Francisco, Ruess penned a very revealing couple of lines that explain much of his behavior regarding taking chances, whether climbing on vertical cliff dwellings or knocking on strangers' doors: "It seems that only in moments of desperation is the soul most truly revealed. Perhaps that's why I am so often so unrestrained, for I always sense the brink of things." His very next letter that May, this time to an unknown recipient, takes this sensing "the brink of things" even further; many would see its darker passages as shading toward the suicidal:

> *Try as I may, I have never yet, that I know of, succeeded in conveying more than a glimpse of my visions. I am condemned to feel the withering fire of beauty pouring into me. I am condemned to the need of putting this fire outside myself and spreading it somewhere, somehow, and I am torn by the knowledge that what I have felt cannot be given to another. I cannot bear to contain these rending flames, and I am helpless to let them out. So I wonder how I can go on living and being casual as one must.*

Though those who met and knew Everett Ruess would find the idea preposterous, the theory of suicide cannot be simply dismissed outright. More than just the above passage supports the theory. A diary entry of September 6, 1933: "I set less and less value on human life, as I learn more about it. I admit the reality of pain in the moment, but its opposite is not as strong. Life does not grip me very powerfully in the present, but I hope it will again. I don't like to take a negative attitude, but it seems thrust upon me." September 15, 1933: "I read about Kanbalu and Khubla Khan, and the hordes of people who lived then. To what end? My interest in life is waning." Though the term was not commonly used in Ruess's time, perhaps he was manic-depressive. Certainly, he did suffer from bouts of deep melancholy.

Whether he died by suicide or unintentional plummet, the reason the mystery remains, of course, is that Everett Ruess's body has never been found. Randolph Jenks, one of the two high schoolers who came across the parched and disoriented Ruess in the Arizona desert, thinks that Ruess was murdered and that his body was thrown into the Colorado River: "I think it was a group of Paiute Indians going up to Escalante for winter supplies, and Everett was coming down." Jenks, now in his nineties, bases this partly on an incident that occurred when he hiked to Rainbow Bridge in the 1930s, and his Navajo guide panicked at seeing some Paiute Indians in the distance. "If they catch us they kill us!" he said. "They kill all strangers." Tad Nichols, Jenks's partner on that trip, also in his nineties, thinks otherwise: "I don't believe he was killed by Indians. He got along well with them. Maybe they didn't like him poking into caves and through their ceremonial material, but I don't think they were responsible." Nichols thinks that Ruess fell into a canyon and was washed away during a flash flood. Both theories, though divergent, would explain the lack of a body. In any case, Jenks still talks of Ruess as a friend, someone who was unique and whom he misses very much. Jenks even accompanied Ruess's brother, Waldo, into Davis Canyon and installed a plaque in Everett Ruess's honor.

Everett's parents earlier made an agonizing, 2,400-mile trip into the desert in June 1935 and visited many of the locations that Everett had written home about. In so doing, they doubtless came to the terrible realization that these places allowed them an understanding of their son that they probably didn't have when he was home, safe, with them. Of course, there was comfort in that as well. Stella Ruess wrote of the desert trip, "We did not expect to find trace of Everett, when so many others had failed, but it gave us great satisfaction to meet these good friends who were so interested. Also to see the wild and gorgeous country he so deeply loved."

Soon after Ruess's disappearance, his parents compiled a collection of his photographs, block prints, essays, letters, poems, and diary excerpts, a project they called "Youth Is for Adventure." This, along with more materials by and about Ruess, was later turned into *On Desert Trails with Everett Ruess* (1940). In the foreword to that book, editor Randall Henderson wrote of Ruess's life, "It was an existence that all imaginative persons dream about—but that few have the will and courage to achieve." In the same volume, Stella included a poem, "Son!" that ends with the line, "Somehow your thoughts are winging through the clouds to me."

It was no doubt excruciatingly painful, but the Ruesses came to accept their son's death. This was helped in great measure by the outpouring of condolences they received after the news of his disappearance. Letters of support and offers of help came from all corners; the townspeople of Escalante massed in helping with searches, and notes from Maynard Dixon, Edward Weston, author Hamlin Garland, and others told of Everett's unique qualities. In fact, the existence of these expressions, plus letters from Everett and photographs of him sent to his parents as potential clues to aid in the search helps explain why entire books filled with writings by and about him exist today. Undoubtedly, the many testimonials as to the unique nature of their son told the Ruesses, if they didn't fully understand it before, that he was truly special. Christopher Ruess wrote to *Desert Magazine* in January 1940, "Whether Everett is alive or dead, he is at peace now. He left us and the world in 20 years more to remember and to treasure than could be required of an average hundred years. We have released him in our hearts to steer by the North Star of his own soul."

In the immediate years after Ruess's disappearance, various sightings of him were reported. One couple, a Mr. and Mrs. MacAntire, Californians vacationing in Utah, claimed that they tried to engage a young man in a conversation near a mine site. The man was unfriendly, snubbing Mrs. MacAntire in a manner that indicated to her that he wished not to be "discovered." When she later learned of the Ruess case, she immediately identified Ruess from photos and maintained that he and the young man who rebuffed her were one and the same.

In 1939, *Desert Magazine* published "Is Everett Ruess in Mexico?" written by Cora Keagle. Mrs. Keagle told the story that in 1937, she and her husband were traveling a few miles south of Monterrey, Mexico, when they came upon two young men trying to fix their stalled automobile. The Keagles gave one of them a ride into town so he could fetch a part for the car. During the ride, the young man explained that he was an artist and had at one time lived with the Indians in Arizona. When Mrs. Keagle later read about Ruess's disappearance in *Desert Magazine* and saw accompanying photos, both she and her husband declared that he was the man they had given the ride to. She ended her letter on this happy note: "[I]f it was Everett he was tanned, healthy and happy and several pounds heavier than when he disappeared."

There were other "sightings," including one in a camp for transients in Florida. But none ever seemed solid enough for further investigation by either Ruess's parents or anyone else. Subsequent searches were limited to the canyon country and repeatedly failed to turn up anything.

Immediately after Ruess's disappearance, his parents attempted to honor his memory by creating The Everett Ruess Poetry Awards, which annually honored two students from Los Angeles High School who submitted original and promising poems. While the awards no longer exist, his memory and influence do. Pulitzer Prize winner N. Scott Momaday once wrote, "Everett Ruess, like Billy the Kid, perpetuates the myth of the dying cowboy . . . that lonely heroic figure who bravely confronts his destiny because he must." The name Everett Ruess still carries currency and is something of a shorthand for those people who believe that adventure, above all else, is why we are here and that the little naggings that hold us back—fear, in essence—must be shunted aside in favor of the unknown; in that way, we can truly live our lives.

In 1997, filmmaker Dyanna Taylor, granddaughter of Dorothea Lange, directed *Vanished!*, a film about Ruess. And in 2000, a feature film, *Lost Forever: Everett Ruess,* directed by Diane Orr, was produced. The Utah towns of Escalante and Boulder host the annual Escalante Canyons Arts Festival, and since 2004, Everett Ruess Days has been a large part of the celebration. Artists compete for prize money, and arts and crafts that Ruess pursued are on display. In late 2006, the Museum of Northern Arizona in Flagstaff held an exhibit titled "Everett Ruess and the Search for Beauty," which featured twenty-six of his wood-block prints. Jerman Design, Inc., out of Salt Lake City, has set up a Web site, www.everettruess.net, which dedicates itself to his writings, artwork, and legend (and offers Everett Ruess merchandise, such as T-shirts and mugs, for sale).

Everett Ruess spent countless evenings by himself, huddled in the warmth of an abandoned Indian dwelling, the smoke from his campfire licking the sides of sandstone cliffs etched with hieroglyphics. Soft rains crept inside and wrinkled the edges of the diary, which he bent toward the fire to write in: "The cave is empty now; the paintings fade. The dim and silent centuries invade."

He once wrote, "Adventure is for the adventurous. My face is set. I go to make my destiny. May many another youth be by me inspired to leave the snug safety of his rut, and follow fortune to other lands." If the continued interest—in some corners, obsessive fascination—is any indication, then this dream, at least, has indisputably come true.

5/ The Aviators: Amelia Earhart and Antoine de Saint-Exupéry

"A saint in short, true to his name, flying up here at the right hand of God. The good Saint-Ex!"

—Tom Wolfe, *The Right Stuff*

"A ghost of aviation / She was swallowed by the sky / Or by the sea, like me she had a dream to fly / Like Icarus ascending / On beautiful foolish arms / Amelia, it was just a false alarm."

—Joni Mitchell, "Amelia"

The sea is shining, it's brilliant, it's the most exquisite ornament on earth, all polish and bangle. It tosses up, slams down, dances back and forth, and folds onto itself in spasms. It's a delight to see from above. But it's also a menace. It draws at the bottom of a low-flying plane. It waits, with tentacles upraised, pulling this heavy piece of machinery. It offers no succor to those in its grasp. Lovers of literature know it well:

> *Water, water, every where,*
>
> *And all the boards did shrink;*
>
> *Water, water, every where,*
>
> *Nor any drop to drink.*
>
> *The very deep did rot: O Christ!*

That ever this should be!

Yea, slimy things did crawl with legs

Upon the slimy sea.

Like Coleridge's Ancient Mariner, we're not sea people; we're so completely out of our element there. We have no fins, no filters, no gills. We dress ourselves in artificial suits and plunge into these alien places, uninvited guests. We thrill at this new world, but we must leave it. This is not our home. We yearn to be flying people; give us wings over flippers any day.

So when the metal bird nosedives, takes its last flight and heads into the abyss of sea, then the wind, the earth, and the stars we know and love all become a world apart, one we will never see again.

How must it feel? What must it be like? Two famed aviators know. Of all people, they know the dangers well. Both had been in crashes before; both had emerged. And what does the survival of such a thing tell us? Does it make us more reverent of the flying machine? The opposite, of course.

Yes, they know it: much is required of the machine. Every mechanical tick must be precise. Man-hours, sweat, time, precision—they must all go toward making this thing right, whole, reliable. But the great Frenchman Antoine de Saint-Exupéry himself warns, "The machine does not isolate man from the great problems of nature but plunges him more deeply into them." In the end, there is only me—at the helm. I am master of this machine. Yes, I know it can all go wrong at any second. Even when it does go wrong, I survive it every time.

But sometimes, the odds must catch up.

Saint-Exupéry once wrote, "When the wild ducks or the wild geese migrate in their season, a strange tide rises in the territories over which they sweep. As if magnetized by the great triangular flight, the barnyard fowl leap a foot or two into the air and try to fly. The call of the wild strikes them with the force of a harpoon and a vestige of savagery quickens in their blood. All the ducks on the farm are transformed for an instant into migrant birds, and into these hard little heads, till now filled with humble images of pools and worms and barnyards,

Lockheed P-38 Lightning similar to the F-5 Lightning that Antoine de Saint-Exupéry was flying when he disappeared

there swims a sense of continental expanse, of the breadth of seas and salt taste of the ocean wind."

So it is with humans. The simple farmer, tilling his field, jerks his head heavenward in amazement at the screaming contraption that slices the sky above him. We all want to fly.

Amelia Earhart was born in 1897 in Atchison, Kansas, on her grandparents' farm. Even though she was restless from the start, the idea of strapping herself into a metal bird and piercing the skies wasn't something that sank into her consciousness for more than twenty years; after all, in an era when the roar of a plane overhead was still a relatively rare occurrence, young Amelia's exposure to aviation would be minimal. But anything mechanical fascinated the young girl, and this allure would never leave her.

When she was twenty-two, Amelia headed to New York, to Columbia University as a premed student. But in a pattern that repeated itself three times, she dropped out, leaving her studies and instead joining the family, now in California.

Here, the fateful event. An aerial show, quite popular in those early days of aviation, was taking place in Long Beach; Amelia and her father attended the show, and she was hooked.

The very next day, she took her first flight—a ten-minute jaunt in an open-cockpit plane. "As soon as we left the ground I knew I myself had to fly!" she later exclaimed. Flying lessons soon followed. Amelia hooked up with another woman flyer—a pioneer in her own right—and the older aviator took the firebrand under her wing, so to speak. Her instructor had initial reservations about Earhart's skill—or lack thereof—but flying was now in her blood. There was no turning back.

Amelia managed to scrape together enough money to buy her own plane, a canary-yellow Kinner. She would burst onto the national consciousness by setting an altitude record in 1922, climbing to fourteen thousand feet. Flying records were being broken as quickly as they were being set, and Amelia Earhart was in on the game. Within a few years, New York publisher George Palmer Putnam wanted to cash in on the aviation craze sweeping the country. Because no woman had ever flown across the Atlantic Ocean, Putnam asked Captain Hilton H. Railey to find a suitable candidate for the stunt. Railey met with Earhart and was struck not so much by her flying expertise as by her physical resemblance to Charles Lindbergh, unquestionably the most famous aviator of the day: "With intense interest I observed and appraised her as she talked. Her resemblance to Colonel Lindbergh was so extraordinary that I couldn't resist the impulse to ask her to remove her hat. She complied, brushing back her naturally tousled, wind-swept hair, and her laugh was infectious. 'Lady Lindy!'"

With Earhart thus stuck with the nickname she detested, the plan was on: Amelia Earhart would be the first woman across the Atlantic in a plane. There was one catch, however, and it didn't sit well with Amelia: she would not be the pilot. "I was a passenger on the journey," she lamented. "Just a passenger." But her disappointment was followed quickly by ambivalence. It became clear after the successful flight that the two male pilots who had pulled it off (no easy feat in 1928) were essentially being ignored by press and well-wishers, who seemed interested only in the woman who had gone along. Earhart wanted the men to receive their due; at the same time, however, she wanted to make the point that she believed that with the right training a woman could do it, too—and do it solo. When the time came for Amelia to fly across the Atlantic by herself, she assured Railey that she was up to it, writing to him: "This is the way I look at it: My family's insured; there's only myself to think about. And when a great adventure's offered you—you don't refuse it, that's all."

Amelia Earhart

Sure enough, she proved herself right. In May 1932, she made her solo traverse of the Atlantic. During the crossing, she had to rapidly descend because of icing on the wings. But she made it, landing near Londonderry, Ireland, from Newfoundland in slightly less than fifteen hours. Afterward, a ticker tape parade was held in her honor in Manhattan, and she received the Distinguished Flying Cross, a very high honor. In Railey's words, the transatlantic flight "turned the whole career of Amelia Earhart—her transformation from an obscure social worker, absorbed in the lives of polyglot gamins at a Boston settlement house, to a world figure in aviation and the honored guest of Kings and Queens."

But she didn't stop, piling up more records and becoming a national darling, an icon in her own age. The records kept on coming: first woman to fly solo round-trip across the United States; altitude records of fifteen thousand feet, then eighteen thousand feet; first to cross the Pacific from Hawaii to California. Everyone from the president to the man on the street wanted a part of the Amelia Earhart mystique. She was, in short, a sensation. And she used her influential position to encourage women to strive for the same heights as she. This was a heady time for American women, who had been granted suffrage only in 1920. And into this new era was thrust a woman who was doing things that even men hadn't yet accomplished. In fact, by the mid-thirties, Earhart's national popularity at least rivaled, if not surpassed, Lindbergh's.

Earhart's stock continued to rise. Physically, she was a somewhat odd mixture of tomboyish competence and feminine allure. She cut her hair short and wore pants and, under her scuffed aviator's jacket, men's shirts. She was often called on to model the newest styles in women's clothing, appearing all over the popular magazines of the day. She became America's darling, a pathfinder, groundbreaker, feminist before the word had the currency it enjoys today. (She also happens to be my daughter's namesake, and it's often the case that on first introduction, people will utter something about flying). But all this was difficult to maintain. The nature of celebrity in America has always been fleeting. Earhart needed to come up with some grand gesture that would cement her place in American history and popular culture. Ultimately, it was Putnam, by this time her husband and manager, who proposed the unthinkable: a round-the-world flight, something so audacious that many observers deemed it virtually impossible. True, a global circumnavigation had been accomplished before, but never by a woman, and never at such a distance; Earhart's route would take her twenty-nine thousand miles more or less along the equator.

Railey apparently had some misgivings about the enterprise, but they came only after the fact: "Long before she mentioned it," he wrote, "I knew that next, and perhaps fatally, must come her globe-circling adventure. Why—when even to her it must have seemed a stunt without constructive benefit to the aeronautical industry—did she attempt the hazardous expedition? She had to. She was caught up in the hero racket which compelled her to strive for increasingly dramatic records, bigger and braver feats that automatically insured the publicity necessary to the maintenance of her position as the foremost woman pilot in the world. She was a victim of the era of 'hot' aeronautics . . ."

The pressure to engage in what many saw as a reckless act was, perhaps, too great to withstand.

Ask anyone in America to name the most famous aviator in history, and you're likely to get one of two answers: Charles Lindbergh or Amelia Earhart. Ask which one went missing, and the answer will invariably come up Earhart.

But ask a European the same question, especially a French-speaking European, and the answer will resound: Antoine de Saint-Exupéry. In North America, his name may ring some bells. It's probable that somewhere along the line, the average American is among the estimated fifty million–plus who have purchased or the millions more who have read *Le Petit Prince* (*The Little Prince)*. The book's stunning success, which has it consistently listed among the most-published books in history, has made "Saint-Ex" a known quantity to lovers of great children's literature. The book has been translated into more than one hundred languages and still sells millions today, some sixty years after its publication. Perhaps a fan of the book is dimly aware that its author was an aviator. But he was more than that. He holds an almost singular place in the history of aviation, and he is, to put it bluntly, a French national hero.

Saint-Ex was a nobleman, a noble man as well, born in 1900 with a name suggesting aristocracy: Jean-Baptiste Marie Roger de Saint-Exupéry, son of Count Jean de Saint-Exupéry, of Lyon, France. Initially interested in architecture, Saint-Ex studied at the École de Beaux-Arts (School of Fine Arts) in Lyon, and then served a stint in the military with the Second Regiment of Chasseurs, a unit of French cavalry whose name translates to "hunters." While in the military, he began his training as a pilot. Flying in the early twenties was an art requiring intense attention to the vagaries of the elements. It was done with a virtual absence of aviation aids inside the cockpit, at least compared to what a commercial pilot enjoys today—enjoyed even just a decade or so after Saint-Exupéry trained. Flying, when Saint-Ex took it up, was an affair run almost entirely on intuition.

With World War I over, the need for pilots focused on new international mail lines servicing France's far-flung colonies, which extended from Western Europe to North and West Africa and Southeast Asia. Saint-Ex began running the postal line for Aéropostale from Toulouse, in southwestern France, to Dakar, Senegal. Because air travel was still in its infancy, every mail flight was potentially fatal; many pilots, for the goal of delivering sacks of letters, never returned home. Saint-Ex wrote of the tenuous state of airmail delivery in his 1931 novel *Night Flight.*

Saint-Exupéry's Aéropostale route took him directly over the massive expanse of the Sahara. This in itself constituted a severe danger; go down in those barren sands, and you might as well count yourself out. In fact, it happened to Saint-Ex and a companion once, on a flight from France to Saigon. The resulting ordeal, chronicled in his extraordinary book *Wind, Sand and Stars,* nearly killed the two men. They were saved on the fourth day after the crash by a Bedouin, whose presence, had it come only a few hours later, would have most probably been too late.

Stationed in North Africa, running the Casablanca-Dakar route, Saint-Ex became enthralled with the Sahara; it would provide the setting for *Le Petit Prince,* which he also illustrated. (So popular was the book that Saint-Exupéry's visage sat side by side with his rendering of the Little Prince on the French fifty-franc note until the conversion to the euro in 2002). Later, Saint-Ex ran the air delivery service at Cape Juby in Western Sahara, near the border with Morocco. The stark beauty of the Sahara stayed with him his entire life, even after he moved to South America in 1929 to oversee Argentina's national airline. For the next decade and a half, Saint-Exupéry wrote and flew, fully engaged in the two vocations that thrilled him most, and the dual areas in which he had few contemporary peers. While World War II raged back home, Saint-Exupéry moved again and was living in comfort on New York's Long Island, in the twenty-two-room Victorian Delamater-Bevin Mansion in Asharoken.

Saint-Exupéry decided that he needed to go back and fight the good fight, though he abhorred war and its senseless destruction. Despite being thirteen years too old for war flight (according to regulation), and being overweight and often inclined to drink, Saint-Exupéry managed to convince the powers that be that he should at least fly reconnaissance, if not direct combat. He got his wish and flew with the Free French GR II/33 squadron doing reconnaissance.

On the evening of July 31, 1944, Saint-Ex took off from his base in Corsica to do recon on German army activity in the Rhône River Valley. The takeoff is a dramatic one, as the craft must slice through the great valleys of Corsica's rugged, mountainous spine. Then the route takes one out to sea, over the Mediterranean.

In *Wind, Sand and Stars,* Saint-Exupéry wrote: "We have all known flights when of a sudden, each for himself, it has seemed to us that we have crossed the border of the world of reality; when, only a couple of hours from port, we have felt ourselves more distant from it than we should feel if we were in India; when there has come a premonition of an incursion into a forbidden world whence it was going to be infinitely difficult to return."

Whether he felt that premonition on that last day in July, we'll never know. But he was never heard from again.

Earhart knew of what Saint-Exupéry wrote. Before her round-the-world flight, she told a friend that she had a vague "feeling" about it. She resolved that it would be her last major flight; afterward, she would settle into a comfortable life spent mostly on the talk and speech circuit. Careful not to label her "feeling" a "premonition," she confided that, "As far as I know, I've only got one obsession—a small and probably feminine horror of growing old—so I won't feel completely cheated if I fail to come back."

She also understood that what many people on the ground saw as pure death-defying stunt work was no less than the advancement of aviation, no small matter. The rest of it was unimportant. Saint-Exupéry knew this as well. He wrote, "I am not talking about living dangerously. Such words are meaningless to me. The toreador does not stir me to enthusiasm. It is not danger I love." Earhart echoed this in an interview she granted the *Huntington Herald-Press* in Indiana: "Aviation is a profession—not a hobby for thrill seekers . . . Never use the word 'thrill' in connection with aviation. Aviators are not thrill seekers. They are men and women interested in their work."

Amelia would be at the controls, but she would not be alone in the plane. Fred Noonan would act as navigator. Noonan, of Irish descent, was a veteran of the First World War and had spent more than two decades at sea on vessels that met with all manner of adventure and mishap. But Noonan also had a reputation as an insufferable drunk. When he was sober, he was the best there was. But when he wasn't, he had an inclination toward instability, something that could be deadly. (However, it should be noted that no evidence exists to suggest that Noonan's penchant for drink played any part in his and Earhart's disappearance). An around-the-world aviation trip would be enough to test anyone's physical limits. But it's worth considering that today's aircraft are infinitely more comfortable and safer than those in Earhart's era. For example, Earhart and Noonan had to exchange notes on the end of a fishing pole because the roar of the engines made conversation impossible. (Noonan did his navigation from the back of the plane, behind Earhart.) Even together inside the plane, they would be very much isolated from the rest of the world. Much would rely on the two being in sync.

And things didn't start terribly well. The first leg of the flight—Oakland, California, to Honolulu—was good enough (establishing a speed record, in fact). But taking off from Honolulu's Luke Field, there was an accident. In the words of one eyewitness, "As the plane started to turn there was a sharp report as if a tire had blown out. As this report came, the right side of the plane's landing gear collapsed, snapping the plane in a wide arc amid a shower of sparks." The plane would have to be packed up and repaired. Afterward, there was the public announcement that the direction of the flight would be reversed—now west to east instead of the other way around. Earhart claimed that this was because of seasonal wind patterns.

With a reversed course and a repaired plane, the couple set off once again. The route had them flying from Oakland to Miami, and then San Juan, Puerto Rico. Next it was Venezuela and Brazil, across the Atlantic to West Africa, over the Sahara and northeast Africa and the Middle East, and down into Asia toward Darwin, Australia. From there, the next stop was Lae, New Guinea. It was from Lae that Earhart took her final flight; the intended target was the small Pacific island of Howland, where fuel supplies awaited her for the final two legs back to the West Coast of the United States.

While Earhart's progress had been tracked by the United States government and amateur short-wave radio operators all along the way, contact with Earhart petered out somewhere on that last flight.

"We are on the line of position 157–337. Will repeat message. We will repeat this message on 6210 kilocycles. Wait. Listening on 6210 kilocycles. We are running north to south." These were Amelia Earhart's last recorded words.

It would be more than fifty years after his disappearance before any word on Saint-Exupéry's whereabouts surfaced. In 1998, a fisherman working just south of the Mediterranean port city of Marseille found a silver bracelet that carried the engraved names of Saint-Exupéry's wife, Consuelo, and his book publishers, Reynal & Hitchcock, of New York. Bits of seaweed and Saint-Exupéry's army uniform were attached. Problem was, the bracelet was found more than one hundred miles from where Saint-Exupéry should have been on that fateful mission. Because of Saint-Exupéry's iconic status in France, the story of the recovered bracelet was roundly dismissed as a ruse. Even Saint-Exupéry's descendants scoffed at it, condemning the fisherman as a prankster. But the piece of jewelry was later identified positively as Saint-Exupéry's. Further, a professional diver named Luc Vanrell found plane wreckage in the very spot where the bracelet was found. The invective about hoaxes and false hope was then turned on Vanrell, and it came from all quarters: not only the family, but also the French press and even French politicians. In fact, the government closed off the area to further searches.

Why was there so much resistance? Vanrell publicly suggested that the great pilot had intentionally plunged his plane into the sea; his being so far off course, and evidence proving that the plane had hit the water vertically, suggested that Saint-Exupéry wasn't shot down by the German Luftwaffe.

What is often forgotten about Saint-Exupéry's final years is that he had had a falling-out with French President Charles de Gaulle, who publicly branded him a traitor and accused him of colluding with the Germans. Even though the charge was roundly dismissed, it stung Saint-Exupéry badly, and his last few months were often spent inebriated and sullen. He had once even muttered, "I shall end up a cross in the Mediterranean."

Even at his best, Saint-Exupéry was frequently close to being overcome with the weight of human misery. His writings are suffused with a love of humanity, despair over the senselessness of human destruction, and a palpable feeling of utter frustration at being unable to convince the whole of civilization of its shared humanity.

There, in the midst of a wretched war, only decades after the "Great War," even fighting on the side of righteousness, he probably couldn't help but be overcome by the uselessness of it all, the intractability of man's terror upon man.

Suicide is a plausible explanation, but it's one that's hard to accept for many French nationals. The war saw the carving of their country, the rise of the Vichy, the required bailout by America and Great Britain. What would it mean if one of the country's favorite sons, hailed after the war as a bona fide hero, had voluntarily checked out?

It may prove impossible to explain Saint-Exupéry's fate. But what has been solved, apparently and after considerable delay, is the mystery of where the great pilot ended up. After his bracelet was found and diver Vanrell recovered the pieces of aircraft in the same area, years went by before the French Ministry of Culture's Department of Subaquatic and Submarine Archaeological Research began testing the wreckage. Among the hundreds of pieces scattered about the seafloor was a tailpiece with the serial number 2734. U.S. Air Force records listed Saint-Exupéry's Lockheed F-5 Lightning as having the same serial number; archives from Lockheed confirmed it.

On April 7, 2004, the Culture Ministry announced that it had proof positive that the plane was Saint-Exupéry's. But while tests on the plane's remains had solved one mystery—where did the great Saint-Ex get off to?—it failed to solve an even greater, and perhaps unsolvable, mystery: why did he go down?

Experts agree that the plane hit the sea vertically, which means that it's very unlikely the plane was shot down. That would have caused it to hit horizontally. Besides, no evidence of bullet holes has been found. While suicide has been suggested, others, including members of Saint-Exupéry's family, speculate that he probably failed to regulate his oxygen and ran out, rendering him unconscious and unaware as the plane made its steady descent into the Mediterranean.

The recovered pieces of Saint-Exupéry's plane now sit in the Museum of Air and Space, outside Paris. The permanent exhibit draws thousands of visitors each year and ensures Saint-Exupéry's place as a legend in French culture and history. In the words that accompany the exhibit, it is "une exposition permanente consacrée au 'père' du Petit Prince" ("a permanent exhibition dedicated to the father of the Little Prince"), and it describes the man himself as "Le pilote, l'artiste et le pionnier de l'aéropostale"—"the pilot, the artist, and the airmail pioneer."

In another nod to the enduring appeal of the man and his wonderful story of the little prince, in 2003 an asteroid moon was named Petit Prince, linking his most famous character astronomically with its creator: 2578 Saint-Exupéry, a main-belt asteroid discovered in 1975. Celestial space is the perfect place for enduring legends.

Earhart and Noonan took off from Lae on July 2, 1937, at 10:20 in the morning. The flight would encompass 2,500 miles to Howland Island, a flyspeck in the Pacific, where the U.S. government had carved out a runway for the express (stated) purpose of aiding Earhart's flight. People on the ground maintained contact for the first 750 miles until radio reception was lost. Roughly 800 miles into the flight, the plane was spotted over the Nukumanu Islands, part of the Melanesian Archipelago off the Solomon Islands and New Guinea. The U.S. Coast Guard cutter *Itasca* waited at Howland, anticipating communication with Earhart and ready with fuel and supplies.

But most analysts agree that sometime after passing the Nukumanu Islands, Earhart strayed off course; hours of failed attempts at communicating with the *Itasca* made finding her way back almost impossible. Worse, by nightfall, a major storm had developed. If Earhart managed to go around it, such maneuvering would have required a large amount of fuel.

Finally, at a quarter to three in the morning, Chief Radioman Leo Bellarts picked up Amelia's voice on the radio. An hour later, they heard her again: "Earhart. Overcast." Radiomen aboard the *Itasca* repeatedly asked for her position and her estimated time of arrival on Howland; each time they were met with silence. When they did hear her again, it was not responses to their queries, but rather static-filled reports about the weather. By a quarter after six, however, her voice came in more clearly. But it was obvious that she couldn't hear the *Itasca*. Half an hour later, she reported that she was a hundred miles out of Howland and would await the *Itasca*'s report. Another hour passed, with Earhart apparently still awaiting word from the *Itasca*. She reported, "We must be on you but cannot see you but gas is running low." Men on the ground calculated her gas reserve at half an hour remaining.

The *Itasca*'s radio operators began frantically broadcasting on different channels, trying desperately to reach her. To no avail: "Earhart calling *Itasca*. We are circling but cannot hear you," she reported. To make matters worse, Earhart didn't give her precise position or her estimated time of arrival, so even though those aboard the *Itasca* could hear her, they had no leads on where to go to try to find her. At 8:44, her final words: "We are running north to south."

In all, more than four thousand people were involved in the search effort—a massive affair that included ten ships, sixty-six airplanes, and a two-hundred-fifty-square-mile search area. It lasted more than two weeks at a cost exceeding four million dollars. It was the most far-reaching search effort in the history of the United States. Despite all the effort, the searchers found nothing.

Official U.S. government reports conclude that because Earhart and Noonan were unable to locate Howland Island, they eventually ran out of fuel waiting for signals from the *Itasca* and then crashed into the deep Pacific, sinking to the bottom some seventeen thousand feet below the surface. Most estimates have the presumed final crash site ranging from roughly thirty to one hundred miles off Howland Island.

Earhart's husband finally returned home from the site after nine days. According to a *San Francisco Chronicle* article dated July 11, 1937, "George Palmer Putnam, husband of the aviatrix, abandoned the sleepless vigil he has maintained since the last message came from the plane a week ago Friday and departed for his home in North Hollywood." Putnam would continue to aid in search efforts for another three months before giving up hope.

In the last letter she ever wrote her husband, Earhart penned these words: "Please know that I am quite aware of the hazards. Women must try to do things as men have tried. When they fail, their failure must be but a challenge to others." It must have been little comfort to Putnam; posterity, history, and groundbreaking feats are one thing when they remain abstractions and when they attain the weight of decades. But when it is one's spouse who perishes in the process, all those lofty ideals must count for little.

The U.S. government search and final report should have been the end of the story—tragic, but generally accepted. But because no confirmed trace of Earhart, Noonan, or their plane has ever been found, theories abound. Randall Brink, in his book *Lost Star: The Search for Amelia Earhart,* is one of many people who maintain that Earhart was on a spying mission for the U.S. government as World War II loomed. Brink lays out his case with this prefatory claim: "Consider simple logic: people and airplanes do not vanish without a trace. Yet not a sliver of airplane wreckage or debris, no scrap of metal or paper, no oil slick, no human remains, or any other tangible evidence of a ditching at sea was ever found."

According to Brink and like-minded theorists, the U.S. government considered Earhart the perfect tool—she was a woman, still something to be taken as rather innocent in those days, and her international celebrity guaranteed cooperation as she flew over otherwise hostile areas where U.S.

government aircraft would never be allowed to fly unmolested. Part of the government's plan, the thinking goes, was to build an airstrip on Howland Island, which would have given the United States a perfect place to launch war maneuvers versus the Japanese if such actions became necessary (which, of course, they did). Developing an airfield in that location without the pretext of the Earhart flight would have been considered by the Japanese to be an act of aggression. Even if the Japanese did suspect that Earhart was involved in some type of reconnaissance, they would certainly think twice before shooting her down. Not only would they have to contend with the world's adoration for her, but also she (and, by extension, the American government) could reasonably argue that she was simply off course—something not at all beyond the realm of possibility.

In fact, some have suggested that Earhart was supposed to get herself intentionally "lost" somewhere near the Marshall Islands. Then, the U.S. Navy would have to retrieve her, giving it an opportunity to spy on the Japanese-held Marshalls. As an ancillary to this theory, many people maintain that Earhart did in fact get to the Marshall Islands, was caught by the Japanese, was taken to the island of Saipan, and was held captive there at least until the end of World War II.

In the years after the disappearance of Earhart and Noonan, several Saipan islanders came forward with tales of two downed fliers taken captive by the Japanese. One woman, Josephine Akiyama, told her story in 1960; it so intrigued veteran CBS broadcaster Fred Goerner that he traveled to Saipan to research Earhart's story. His 1966 book, *The Search for Amelia Earhart,* recounts his findings. Even though decades had passed, several people on the island, once prisoners of the Japanese Imperial Army, claimed to have seen a white woman, described as a pilot and "looking like a man, with men's clothes and short hair," sitting despondent in a cell. Goerner claimed further proof: he discovered government documents suggesting that fliers had indeed been picked up and executed. But such claims cannot be proven. Further, it must be noted that Saipan, in the Northern Mariana Islands, sits some 1,500 miles from Howland, a distance that would have meant that Noonan and Earhart were extremely off course. Some have argued that the two were captured in the Marshall Islands and then spirited to Saipan. But this would still put them hundreds of miles off course, which doesn't jibe with Earhart's last transmissions heard by the *Itasca.* Also, no pieces of aircraft recovered in and around Saipan have turned out to be Earhart's, and various discoveries of bones around the island have also come up negative.

Other theories abound: Earhart was indeed captured by the Japanese, but instead of being executed, she was forced to broadcast Japanese propaganda to American servicemen in the Pacific Theater during World War II; she lived as a castaway for many years on a Pacific island with native fisherman; she actually was recovered by the American government, which was so embarrassed by the whole business that it ferried her home to New Jersey, where she lived many years under an assumed identity.

The existence of such divergent theories is not surprising, considering that the mythologizing began almost immediately. In 1943, a film, *Flight for Freedom,* presented a barely veiled story about a woman aviator on a spying mission for the American government. The pilot in the film was a carbon copy of Amelia Earhart. One organization, The International Group for Historic Aircraft Recovery (TIGHAR), has dedicated many resources to finding out what happened to Earhart and Noonan, as well as separating fact from fiction. For example, of the Japanese capture theory, TIGHAR maintains, "Allegations that Earhart and her navigator had been captured by the Japanese were investigated and found to be groundless by both U.S. Army Intelligence and the United Press as early as 1949." TIGHAR also flatly dismisses the various claims of secret U.S. government documents.

The hypothesis that TIGHAR supports actually hews closely to the American government's initial position in 1937: Earhart crash-landed and sent distress calls from some unknown island for days before she and Noonan succumbed to injury, toxic food, or thirst. While the U.S. government eventually dismissed those distress calls as either "hoaxes or misunderstandings," TIGHAR maintains that Earhart actually went down in the Phoenix Islands, now part of the island nation of Kiribati, which sits southeast of Howland Island on a bearing of 157 degrees. In fact, the heel of a woman's shoe and bits of airplane wreckage have been found on Nikumaroro Island, part of the Phoenix group—but none of this has been confirmed to have belonged to Earhart.

Undeterred, members of TIGHAR are currently in the process of raising funds for another expedition to the area, believing that the bones of Earhart might very well be yet recovered somewhere on the island. Perhaps bits of airplane wreckage may yet still be salvaged as well.

Men and women sometimes disappear. They die, and they leave us. When they are famous, their lives become stories to be marveled at, and at each retelling, the actual person, the human being, gets farther and farther from us, assuring that he or she becomes more and more lodged in a consciousness that winds up being more false than real.

Amelia Earhart disappeared; her story continues to perplex, and inspire. Antoine de Saint-Exupéry also vanished. They are both gone now, and with them entire universes. Theirs were outsize personalities, and they became known as icons impossible to live up to in actuality. But they were people, too, and as such were entire worlds unto themselves. It must be remembered that even the dregs of humanity take with them the whole of the planet when they go. Writing of the killed miner and the lowly slave, Saint-Ex put it this way:

Inside the narrow skull of the miner pinned beneath the fallen timber, there lives a world. Parents, friends, a home, the hot soup of evening, songs sung on feast days, loving kindness and anger, perhaps even a social consciousness and a great universal love, inhabit that skull. By what are we to measure the value of a man? His ancestor once drew a reindeer on the wall of a cave; and two hundred thousand years later that gesture still radiates. It stirs us, prolongs life in us. Man's gestures are an eternal spring. Though we die for it, we shall bring up that miner from his shaft. Solitary he may be; universal he surely is . . . When a man dies, an unknown world passes away. I could not tell what visions were vanishing in the dying slave, what Senegalese plantations or white Moroccan towns. It was impossible for me to know whether, in this black heap, there was being extinguished merely a world of petty cares in the breast of a slave—the tea to be brewed, the camels watered; or whether, revived by a surge of memories, a man lay dying in the glory of humanity. The hard bone of his skull was in a sense an old treasure chest; and I could not know what colored stuffs, what images of festivities, what vestiges, obsolete and vain in this desert, had here escaped the shipwreck.

Of course, this is no less—and no more—true of Saint-Ex and Amelia as well.

Saint-Exupéry wrote in *Wind, Sand and Stars*, "I know nothing, nothing in the world, equal to the wonder of nightfall in the air. Those who have been enthralled by the witchery of flying will know what I mean—and I do not speak of the men who, among other sports, enjoy taking a turn in a plane. I speak of those who fly professionally and have sacrificed much to their craft. Mermoz [a pilot friend] said once, 'It's worth it, it's worth the final smash-up.'"

Amelia Earhart once said, "When I go, I would like to go in my plane. Quickly." Perhaps it was bravado, or an easy thing to say when such an outcome was still just a possibility and not a reality, but we must take her at her word. We can only hope that Amelia truly felt the same way as Saint-Exupéry's friend Mermoz; we can hope that both aviators, blazers across the early sky, managed a smile at the end. We can hope that, indeed, it was worth it.

6/

Lost Scion: Michael Rockefeller

There are all kinds of creatures that can kill a human. Though we often think of the alphas—lions, tigers, rhinos, hippos, elephants—most of the human-killers are smaller than we are. There's something poetic about this fact. After all, humans, for all our glories, have exacted one serious toll on the earth and its organisms. If the occasional spider or scorpion or snake gets one for its side, that seems entirely reasonable.

It's something of a comfort (or a horror, depending on your view) that we may be eaten afterward. At least—so the comforting side goes—we have supplied some necessity to our killer(s). But what if you were going to feed a fellow human being? Being eaten by a crocodile or a shark is enough to inspire fear in anyone, but the prospect of being eaten by another person involves such utter revulsion as to be almost incomprehensible. We don't expect rationality from a shark; we expect primal impulse. From a crocodile, we anticipate savagery, even if that's mostly humans projecting our own fears and irrationality. But fellow humans, part of the brotherhood of mankind? We don't look into a gleaming eye and expect to get lip-licking anticipation in return. None of us would, especially someone who was born into the sort of privilege few people on earth can even comprehend.

Did the inheritor of a billion-dollar estate meet his end in this most gruesome manner? It sounds like a lame party joke: "Which is worst? Getting eaten by a crocodile, a shark, or a cannibal?"

Michael Rockefeller's great-grandfather, John D., founded Standard Oil and retired in 1911 with the equivalent in today's economy of billions of dollars. John's grandson Nelson was a politician, a four-term Republican governor of New York and a presidential hopeful, eventually ascending to the vice presidency under Gerald Ford. It was into this family that Michael Rockefeller was born, a boy of privilege who would eventually go to Phillips Exeter and Harvard.

Aside from guaranteeing the elite schooling, Rockefeller's birth into that famous family assured another thing that would influence his short life: exposure to art, and in particular "primitive" art. Father Nelson was a trustee of the Metropolitan Museum of Art, among others. The museum venture that would most influence his son was Nelson's founding of the Museum of Primitive Art in 1954, seven years before Michael would head off to one of the remotest places on earth to collect indigenous art that would eventually make its way into the museum's collection.

Michael Rockefeller was born in 1938. Early photos show a somewhat nerdy kid, his face dominated by large spectacles, but Michael Rockefeller was no milquetoast; he blossomed into a sturdy man of more than six feet. He did a stint in the military, and while he had access to his family's far-flung and exotic properties, he often stayed at them doing menial jobs, wishing to feel something of what life was like outside the safety net of extraordinary wealth and privilege. In Puerto Rico, Michael spent a summer bagging groceries, and he worked as a ranch hand at the Rockefeller ranch in Venezuela.

But it would be his venture in 1961, at age twenty-three, that would prove his most daring and adventuresome.

The world's second-largest island, New Guinea is just north of Australia, tantalizingly close to the northernmost point of Cape York, but it's a world away from anywhere. Even today, the interior highlands of New Guinea are about as remote and inaccessible as one can get on this earth. An adventurous person can sign on to a "first contact" tour to meet tribes that have allegedly

Michael Rockefeller

never seen white people. Its inhabitants speak a dizzying array of languages—more than eight hundred by last count, making it one of the most linguistically diverse places on earth.

Its enticingly exotic name comes from a Spanish explorer who saw similarities between the natives and those he had seen in Guinea, in West Africa. Earlier, a Portuguese explorer named the island Ilhas dos Papuas, which, roughly translated, means the "island of the frizzy-haired." Western colonists weren't too far behind. Apparently, they weren't sufficiently put off by wild accounts of the place. In 1888, the French explorer Louis Tregance published *Adventures in New Guinea,* which contained descriptions of his captivity by a tribe called the Orangwoks, who, among other eccentricities, used yellow-striped ponies as their main mode of conveyance.

The Netherlands eventually "settled" and exerted colonial control over the western half of the country, dubbing it Netherlands New Guinea. The eastern half was ruled by the English and Germans and later was administered by the Australians after that country's independence from England. While the English and Australians established cities where they installed Westerners, by and large the mountainous interior was left alone and virtually uncharted. A ridge of mountains runs along the entire island, rising in some spots to nearly fifteen thousand feet. Horrendous weather makes this a dicey area to fly over. The mountains shuttle the frequent rains down a series of rivers that run to the mangrove-laced coasts. This onrush of water also creates some unstable sea conditions around the island, most notably on the Casuarina Coast, along the southwest.

The island has had a tumultuous political history. Today, it's split right down the middle into sovereign Papua New Guinea in the east and two Indonesian provinces in the west. But when Rockefeller was tooling around the island in 1961, it was caught in the grip of a lot of bellicose push and pull, becoming the conflict point in brinksmanship between the Netherlands and Indonesia. Initially, this struggle had comparatively little to do with the usual historical explanations for colonial geographic fights: exploitation of native labor, accessing of natural resources, or furthering of imperial pride and importing of "civilization." (Though it has been argued that eventually both the Dutch and the Indonesians would put some combination of all three into effect.) For the Dutch, New Guinea stood at a geographically strategic point for shoring up their old Dutch East Indies trading empire. For the newly independent Indonesia, the large island just off its eastern shores stood in its direct sphere of influence, and having the old colonial master so close by was a distasteful prospect. Besides, New Guinea—the western half at least—would prove a perfect place for undesirable castoffs from overpopulated Indonesian cities.

Before all of this fighting and dividing, the island had already developed a unique, and to the western world horrifying, reputation. In 1877, a Scottish missionary named James Chalmers set up shop in inland New Guinea at the behest of the London Missionary Society. He spent a quarter century creating missionary posts in some incredibly remote and inhospitable regions of the island, where native tribes toiled in Stone Age conditions and where they had certainly never seen white faces before. In 1901, both Chalmers and an aide were attacked, killed, and then eaten by head-hunting, cannibalistic tribes. The case made international news and cemented New Guinea's reputation as an outpost of extraordinary savagery. A half century later, the practices of head-hunting and cannibalism remained in full force. Because of this, anthropological teams after World War II set off in droves to the island, which they regarded as a perfect laboratory for studying uncontacted and "unspoiled" tribes.

In late 1960, while Rockefeller was a student at Harvard, the university's Peabody Museum of Archaeology and Ethnology announced plans to sponsor an expedition to New Guinea to study the Dani tribe. A professor of anthropology, Robert Gardner, would lead the expedition. A young and rising star at Harvard, Gardner already had a film credit for a documentary on the Kalahari Bushmen.

Rockefeller once wrote, "It's the desire to do something adventurous at a time when frontiers, in the real sense of the word, are disappearing." It was to New Guinea that the young heir went in search of that disappearing frontier. It was there where he got more than he bargained for.

Rockefeller, though interested in native art and in archaeology, didn't have the expertise required for such an expedition. He did, however, have the birth name of Rockefeller. He would go, provided he paid his own way. (It was later surmised that the Rockefeller family paid much of the expedition's costs, as well. In fact, there was initially some Dutch resistance to the entire expedition. But, as a testament to Nelson Rockefeller's power and influence, he called high-ups in both Washington and Amsterdam and got everything cleared and ready to proceed.) Michael's position would be that of "sound technician," meaning that he would hold the microphone as the team recorded film of natives in the remote Baliem Valley. (It would be suggested that "any dope could hold a microphone." Translation: no one was under any illusions as to how Rockefeller got there.)

Among others on the expedition was Peter Matthiessen, who would eventually gain fame for his nature writings, including the National Book Award–winning *The Snow Leopard*. The famously hearty Matthiessen was unsure about Rockefeller, sensing that if things got too difficult, the spoiled rich boy would pack up and head home: "That was always a possibility . . . he quoted Dad a lot . . . and we kind of knew that he was sponsoring the expedition." But Michael would ultimately prove extremely adept at photography. His black-and-white stills of the native population were very good, eventually being collected in *The Asmat*, edited by Dutch anthropologist Adrian Gerbrands.

But this too caused some friction on the expedition. Matthiessen explained, "He simply wasn't doing the job. He got some sound and what he got was OK. It just wasn't enough . . . he was off photographing when he should have been taking sound." Matthiessen would eventually soften his tone toward Rockefeller, perhaps seeing the insulation of the Rockefeller name to be a hindrance as much as a free pass. In Matthiessen's 1962 book, *Under the Mountain Wall: A Chronicle of Two Seasons in Stone Age New Guinea*, he included Rockefeller in the book's dedication: "In warm memory of Michael Rockefeller, whose interest and generosity were a major contribution to the Harvard-Peabody expedition of 1961." Rockefeller's photographs also grace the book's pages.

Nevertheless, at the time, the other members of the expedition found Rockefeller a bit too insulated from the real world. True, he was there with the rest of them, sweating it out and trying desperately to abate the mosquitoes, but he had grown up in extraordinary privilege, something, to their minds, that automatically skewed his sense of reality. One day, the expedition members had a late-night meeting and really laid into Rockefeller for not getting enough recorded sound. (No doubt, some of the team members enjoyed the novelty of busting the chops of a man worth many millions of dollars.) According to Matthiessen, Michael left in tears but came around the following morning and turned into a more mature, more conscientious member. Additionally, what no one could deny was that Michael had a real aptitude as a photographer. He hadn't any formal training, but when the expedition photos were compiled for a book, *Gardens of War*, it was clear that Michael was the best photographer of the team.

Blossoming into an indispensable member of the team was necessary. After all, this Harvard party was no colonial-style expedition with native porters carrying litters of sun-baked Westerners. Many of the tribes native to the Baliem Valley were still living on the edge of the Stone Age. The valley itself sits in a crest some five thousand feet in altitude, surrounded by soaring peaks rising to thirteen thousand feet. Rockefeller's description: "The Baliem is a thing of magnificent vastness, decorated with the greens of the valley floor and the blues of the surrounding mountains. The mountains rise often a great deal over 10,000 feet on all sides and are constantly hidden and altered by the clouds that gather about them." First missionary contact with the Dani tribe in the Baliem wasn't made until the mid-1950s, just seven years before the Harvard expedition—it was a place that was potentially very hostile to outsiders. Plus, this was one of the more inhospitable climes that any of the expedition participants would ever see. Crushing humidity, nasty mosquitoes, and punishing rain showers that turned everything to rot: these were the conditions the expedition endured for a full half year. In short, it was an unlikely place to find a billionaire's son. But it was the kind of place that suited Rockefeller's restless spirit. Many who knew Michael Rockefeller during his short life attested to his constant need to prove himself, to show all those around him that he was no spoiled brat, that he had the fortitude to take on difficulties and deal with them head-on. Choosing to go to New Guinea was no coincidental, happy accident. It would be the perfect proving ground. But New Guinea was no place to prove one's mettle against common-sense warnings.

The expedition's time in New Guinea would lead to the production of the documentary film *Dead Birds,* now considered an ethnographic classic. The film spotlights the Dani, who proved to be a fierce people, believing firmly in revenge murder; when one of their own was killed by a neighboring tribe, there would have to be revenge exacted. Of course, this could go on in perpetuity. Because this characteristic was of singular interest to ethnographers, the expedition would hit the jackpot if a war broke out; they might even be able to film a head-hunting ceremony. As it turned out, the team was repeatedly disappointed that no full-scale war broke out and that no casualties were taken. Nevertheless, signs of the ferociousness of Dani culture were everywhere, and Rockefeller dutifully recorded them with his camera; a particularly chilling example was the large number of women walking around with missing fingers. As homage to dead relatives, women hacked off a digit. Large numbers of fingerless women wearing necklaces of shriveled phalanges was testament to the repetition of war among the Dani.

When expedition leader Gardner first landed on New Guinea, he stopped at the colonial capital at Hollandia (now Jayapura), where Dutch government representatives showed him some native art. Among the items that impressed him most were *bis* poles, which are something like totem poles. There is one significant difference, however: while North American natives used totem poles exclusively for storyboards and ancestor worship, the Asmat tribes along the southeastern coast of New Guinea carved the *bis* poles for gorier reasons.

Bis poles can stand some twenty feet in height, topped by the carved representation of a dead ancestor. The figure is invariably outfitted with well-endowed genitalia and more often than not holds an intricate, almost lacy wood carving of what appears to be another, much larger penis above the human-scaled one, suggesting what awaited him in the afterlife. But before that spirited fun could ensue, this ancestor's death had to be avenged. (And, it has been noted, virtually no one in Asmat lore dies of natural causes. Even the most seemingly benign visitations of death were caused by some black magic.) The carving of a *bis* pole is a promise to the unavenged ancestor. When the ceremony surrounding the *bis* pole was complete and the person had been avenged, the pole was either chucked into the river or dragged into the forest and left for the insects and moisture to do their decaying work.

Gardner's description of the Asmat art intrigued Rockefeller, who arranged to take a side trip to the southern coast to see the poles—and other artifacts—for himself. He met his friend and Harvard roommate Sam Putnam, who was joining the expedition late. Together, the two of them scoured the Asmat areas along the coast for good art, and then headed back to the Baliem Valley to rejoin the expedition and see it to its end. This trip did present one potential danger, however. The Asmat had a reputation for being particularly violent and hostile. Despite this, Rockefeller reported no problems in his visit; in fact, he was somewhat smitten by the Asmat, and by one point in particular. He wrote, "As remarkable as the art is the fact that the culture which produced it is still intact; some remote areas are still headhunting; and only five years ago, almost the whole area was headhunting." Putnam, too, didn't remember there being any sense that at any minute the head-hunting Asmat would set on them, tie them to a spit, and make them the evening's meal. Instead, his recollections centered more on the extraordinary natural force of the Asmat homeland: "[B]lack, black water, and the trees arching above our heads forming this canopy and the roots coming out of the water forming these great arches. And the birds. It was just spectacular."

Aside from the *bis* poles, Michael took a personal interest in Asmat skulls. Head-hunting among the Asmat was used to establish social order and tribal hierarchy, both internally and externally. Usually, a killed tribe member was avenged, and the new victim's head would become a trophy of sorts for the vanquisher. The skulls were often placed on posts around the village. However, other skulls, mostly of dead ancestors, took up hallowed places within homes; some accounts have tribesmen smoking tobacco out of hollowed skulls and even using them as pillows for nighttime sleep. But some skulls received even more special treatment.

These skulls, among the Asmat tribes' greatest artistic creations, received precise preparation. Each skull contained the telltale hole near the temple where the brains were extracted for consumption. The heads then were set to cook, the flesh slowly peeling away and being eaten as well. The skull was then placed in the open air to allow any clinging remnants of flesh to rot away and disintegrate. No doubt, in years before colonial control, when natives were free to operate unhindered, the scene after a large raiding party saw dozens of skulls sitting around in various states of decay.

Once completely free of flesh, the skull was fitted with clay to re-create the original contours of the victim's face. The person who had been killed also involuntarily bequeathed his or her hair, and this was reinstalled on top of the skull to approximate as best as possible the original coif. Then the head was painted and given *giri-giri* shells for eyes to round out the likeness. The finished pieces were startlingly realistic, executed with incredible care and diligence. They were extraordinary artifacts, and these were what Rockefeller prized most.

He should have been with the Asmat earlier. In 1956, a raid by Asmat tribesmen resulted in the brutal slayings of almost thirty men, women, and children from a neighboring tribe. Three years later, a massacre took the lives of more than fifty teenage boys; the killers explained to the Dutch investigators that they needed the heads for courting women in the tribe. They added that the boys' meat was young and fresh.

When the expedition in Baliem ended and the team headed back to the States, Michael's fidgety spirit wasn't sated, but instead encouraged: he wanted to go back. This time, he would visit the southern coast and the Asmat to collect art for the Museum of Primitive Art. Two years earlier, he had been named a trustee of the museum—what an opportunity to fill its halls with art he had personally collected.

While Michael was home, his father gave him news that depressed him terribly: his parents would be getting divorced. Michael was close with both his mother and father, and he found the news devastating. It did, however, make his decision to return to New Guinea even firmer. It would be virtually impossible to be farther away from the unpleasantness at the family manse.

Back in New Guinea, Rockefeller made contact with the Asmat tribes. He was as taken with the Asmat *bis* poles as Robert Gardner had been, noting, "This was the one kind of object that seemed inviolate for the encroachment of Western commercialism upon Asmat art." And this point must be noted: it would incredibly unfair, downright inaccurate in fact, to paint Rockefeller as a crass collector bent on fattening his haul at the expense of decorum or proper respectful gesture. Rockefeller had a genuine interest in collecting the art to showcase back home for the main purpose of educating the West as to the nobility and craftsmanship of these people who were too easily dismissed as uncivilized and cannibalistic headhunters.

When Rockefeller witnessed what he perceived to be the ugly encroach-ment of Western values on the natives, he often noted it in his diaries and journals. On one early trip to the village of Omadesep, his idyll was broken suddenly by a horrible realization: "How marvelous the approach as we glided over the water abreast the four canoes that had come to welcome us. The river opened up revealing the large village that lines both sides of the river. Yet then how discouraging to find that the large wooden building on the east bank was a school. The class was in session and the monotonous chant of the Roman alphabet greeted our approach." Later, he wrote: "The Asmat is filled with a kind of tragedy. For many of the villages have reached that point where they are beginning to doubt the worth of their own culture and crave things Western. There is everywhere depressing respect for the white man's shirt and pants, no matter how tattered or dirty; even though these doubtful symbols of another world seem to hide a proud form and replace a far finer, if less concealing, form of dress." Of course, what Rockefeller was describing was grinding poverty. It's easy to lament the loss of a "pure" culture mired in poverty when you get to go back home to relative splendor. And Rockefeller's "relative splendor" was off the charts.

Rockefeller spent his days arranging travel up and down rivers and into villages, and setting up trades, using the village of Agats as his base for storing his newly acquired goods. One particular village of interest because of its size—and its corresponding treasure of artifacts—was Otsjanep. Other coastal villagers feared this village; Otsjanep men had a fierce reputation. They had been unbridled and successful headhunters just a few years prior to Rockefeller's visit, and while the Dutch officially claimed that the practice had been successfully suppressed, that claim was disputable.

Rockefeller wasn't alone when he went to such places as Otsjanep; the Dutch authorities assigned him a companion to help navigate his way. Rockefeller's partner was a taciturn Dutch anthropologist named Rene Wassing. Ostensibly, Wassing was the "expert," the guy to successfully navigate the often-awkward exchanges between the Asmat and the white men. To Rockefeller, Wassing was perfect. He often kept quiet and retained a northern European reserve, even a detachment, on most all matters. This allowed Rockefeller to operate virtually unfettered. While this may have been a good thing for Rockefeller and the life he was living at the moment, it would have grave implications later.

Rockefeller's sometimes forceful personality (developed, no doubt, by the fact that in the end he really could have anything he wanted) didn't fly among the expedition members. But more or less on his own on the southern coast, he could ignore advice at will. And, apparently, this is exactly what he did. A Dutch patrol officer in Agats had warned Rockefeller about the extremely strong and dangerous tides and currents that bedeviled that part of the coast. Rockefeller evidently wasn't interested. On his initial visit to the area, he had traversed the very places he was later warned about, and things had gone off without complication. Why shouldn't they be the same now? Besides, one thing that Michael Rockefeller could rightly claim was that he was a very strong swimmer. Should he actually find himself dumped in the water, he had every confidence in his ability to get either to shore or back to his vessel.

In 1958, a Dutch patrol visited Otsjanep with the intent of trying to quell the village's continued forays into head-hunting and cannibalism. Otsjanep had always had a nasty reputation, and the Dutch went in with guns at the ready.

As they approached, they could see villagers on either side of the river, armed with spears and, at first blush, ready for a battle. Then bursts of smoke appeared over the heads of the villagers; it seemed they had guns of their own! One of the Dutch crew, a Papuan from a different village unused to such displays, lost his nerve and started firing indiscriminately into the villagers.

Apparently, what freaked out the Dutch patrolman was an exhibition by the villagers that only gave the appearance of their possessing firearms. It was an old trick; almost two centuries earlier, when James Cook made a pass along the same coast, he noted the inhabitants standing on the land. He wrote:

> *They made much the same appearance as the New Hollanders, being nearly of the same stature, and having their hair short-cropped: like them also they were all stark naked, but we thought the color of their skin was not quite so dark; this, however, might be the effect of their not being quite so dirty. All this, while they were shouting defiance, and letting off their fires by four or five at a time. What these fires were, or for what purpose intended, we could not imagine: those who discharged them had in their hands a short piece of stick, possibly a hollow cane, which they swung sideways from them, and we immediately saw fire and smoke, exactly resembling those of a musket, and of no longer duration. This wonderful phenomenon*

*was observed from the ship, and the deception was so great, that the
people on board thought they had fire-arms; and in the boat, if we
had not been so near that we must have heard the report, we should
have thought they had been firing volleys.*

In fact, the villagers were simulating gunpowder smoke—to great effect,
obviously. The villagers had earlier been impressed with the white man's show of
power and sought to imitate it. Except that the villagers had no gunpowder—
what they were doing was taking lime powder and throwing it up through
hollow sticks. This was a standard greeting to those who approached tribes by
river. The villagers also waved flags as a sort of choice—you can come in peace,
or you can get the "guns." Problem was, the 1958 Dutch patrol didn't see the
display of flags on the other side of the river. When the incident was over, four
Otsjanep villagers lay dead.

The dead, as we know, must be avenged; otherwise, their spirits will create
havoc for the living. Here's the twist: as the murderer of another, the living
vanquisher becomes the "keeper of the spirit" of the vanquished. Because of this,
the killer cannot be the one who is then killed for that particular deed. If he is,
then the original victim's soul is never properly redeemed. Instead, the person
who pays the price for that other killing will be someone from the same tribe.

The Dutch were white. It's as simple as that; they belonged to Rockefeller's
tribe because, well, he was white, too.

After Michael's disappearance, the Dutch deputy governor of Netherlands New
Guinea stated, "Michael was offering ten steel hatchets for one head. We had
to warn him off because he was creating a demand which could not be met
without bloodshed." As evidence, the deputy governor related a story about
representatives of a head-hunting tribe asking permission, "for one evening
only, please, sir," to go on a raid.

It is of some dispute whether Rockefeller was in fact creating this demand
for fresh heads. After all, he wasn't asking for new ones; he would have
been very satisfied with those existing. Further, the Harvard Peabody team
also had similar charges leveled at it—the Dutch authorities accused the
expedition members of encouraging warfare to meet expectations (and gain
filmed evidence) of war-happy tribes. This provided an easy explanation for

the Dutch as to why these tribes still engaged in such barbarism when public proclamations stated that these nasty habits had been wiped out, evidence of the benign civilizing effect the Dutch were having on New Guinea.

But one example of Rockefeller's poor judgment isn't up for dispute. He received several warnings about the trip he was proposing to take with Wassing across the mouth of the Eilanden River in his thirty-foot catamaran, an awkward sort of pontoon vessel constructed by lashing together two canoes with a bamboo deckhouse and a tin roof for shelter. The vessel was powered by a single, eighteen-horsepower outboard motor. A local patrol officer used a similar vessel because it maneuvered extraordinarily well in the twisting rivers. But for the tough conditions along the coast where Rockefeller planned to travel, the boat was very unsuitable.

Where the Eilanden River meets the Arafura Sea, there's a powerful collision, resulting in waves that can reach twenty feet in height. The onrushing water of the Eilanden shuttling from the highlands crashes into the Arafura. When the sea's tides are rushing toward land, the impact creates a powerful and perilous place to navigate. Islanders knew better than to try; if the conditions created the collision described above, the natives did one of two things: they either hugged the coastline or headed far out into the sea, where the impact didn't reach.

American anthropologist David Eyde, working in the area, warned Rockefeller not to take that boat on those dangerous tides. Eyde noted Rockefeller's obstinacy and surmised, "I had the impression that Michael was awfully used to having his way, not taking advice from anyone." A Dutch trader named Verhey van Wyck, who refused to sell gasoline to Rockefeller in hopes he would reconsider making the trip, echoed this sentiment. After unsuccessfully trying to get Rockefeller to lighten the load in his boat, van Wyck came away with the impression that Michael "had the need to prove himself." Perhaps this was a hangover from getting the business from some of the expedition team members during his earlier trip in the Baliem Valley. Later, a Dutch police officer saw Rockefeller's catamaran sitting very low in the water at Agats because it was grossly overburdened with trade goods. The officer made Rockefeller off-load much of the bulk before he was satisfied. When he left, Rockefeller simply put the materials back in the boat and took off. This is another place where Rene Wassing's reticence proved useful for Rockefeller.

They eventually did set off in their overloaded boat to attempt the Eilanden crossing. But they weren't alone; two native boys, Simon and Leo, who presumably knew well the vagaries of the river, accompanied them. The boys convinced the two Westerners that the sea looked bad and that they should head upriver, hugging the bank, then cross the river at a calmer place and spit back out into the sea on the other side. But as they tried to go upriver, the weight of the boat pushed them too low, and the propeller repeatedly kicked up mud. This forced them back into the middle of the river. There, large, swelling WAves kicked up around them. One swamped the boat and stalled the motor, and the passengers began bailing like mad. Wassing tried to restart the motor, but it had been swamped beyond operation. Wassing described it this way: "A wave came over the stern and side of the boat, stopping the engine and swamping the hulls. We sank visibly and the current continued to push out to sea."

The two boys argued that everyone should jump out and swim for shore, as it wasn't far. But Wassing couldn't swim. So Rockefeller stayed with Wassing, and the boys jumped overboard, promising to get help once they reached shore. Of course, there was no guarantee they *would* reach shore. This was a rough sea, after all, and inhabited by man-eaters, no less.

As the boys swam, they looked back to see that the boat had begun capsizing and Wassing and Rockefeller had climbed onto the tin roof. The two men tried to paddle toward shore, but the current only took them farther out to sea. "It was useless," Wassing said later. "We just had to treat the overturned hulls as a raft and drift where the current was taking us, farther and farther out to sea."

Simon and Leo did ultimately make it to shore; it took a harrowing five-hour swim to do it. Once there, they ran to the nearest village, screaming for help. The search and rescue was on. It began with only Dutch patrol boats running up and down the shore; soon, the government added naval vessels and helicopters. Several days went by before the Dutch accepted mass logistical support from the Americans and Australians. In all, there would be three Neptune search planes and twelve naval vessels in on the hunt. But it didn't stop there; five thousand coastal New Guineans in a thousand canoes were put on the search as well, motivated by the offer of a large quantity of tobacco, promised by Nelson Rockefeller. The scion, it turned out, was worth a fortune here, too.

But on that first day, help did not come fast enough. The two men clung to the remains of their vessel for the entire night. When the first hints of dawn appeared from the inky night, Rockefeller had had enough. He intimated that he might try to swim for it. Wassing finally abandoned his reticence and tried to talk him out of it. There were several good arguments in Wassing's favor: they had drifted far out to sea, and there was no good way to tell how far they were from land; the water, aside from being rough, was full of predators; the first rule of seamanship is to always stay with the boat; and—we can certainly forgive Wassing for this—who the hell wants to be left alone in such a predicament?

"I tried very hard to talk that plan out of his head," Wassing said. "He listened to me, but I knew in advance that he would go ahead. It was always very difficult to make him change his mind . . . He was a brave man, but also very unreasonable."

Finally, Wassing told him, "Michael, I don't take any responsibility for what you are going to do." He later told reporters, "Michael's restless nature made it impossible for him to endure our drifting around."

So Rockefeller, as was his history, got his way. He stripped down to his underwear, tied his glasses around his head with some twine, emptied two jerricans of gasoline and rigged them around his chest as flotation devices, and turned to Wassing.

"I think I can make it," he said. Those, as far as anyone knows, were his last words. He was never seen again, at least officially.

It's true that the Dutch weren't too thrilled with anyone poking around their colonial territory, but allowing small bands of researchers and scientists to study the inland tribes showed that, at least on the surface, the Dutch interests in New Guinea were legitimate and devoted to increased understanding of our world through science and anthropology—certainly lofty and legitimate pursuits. However, a fine balance had to be struck. The fewer people poking around, the better.

Of the four on the boat—Wassing, Rockefeller, and the two natives, Simon and Leo—three survived, and one was never seen again. It was obvious what had happened: Michael Rockefeller had died at sea. This was the official Dutch finding. It did help the Dutch case that many of Rockefeller's actions while he was on the island could be called reckless and irresponsible. It certainly took some heat off the Dutch that they could point out, rightly, that Rockefeller had ignored all good advice and attempted to cross the Eilanden in a dangerously overloaded boat at the worst possible time of day. They hoped that no one would think that the Dutch had at least some indirect complicity in this. Rockefeller's experience in New Guinea was limited mostly to the interior

Baliem Valley; he had spent little time on the coast. While this was certainly no fault of the Dutch, they did assign a minder, Rene Wassing, who himself had almost as little experience as Rockefeller. In short, the two were ill-equipped for what they were headed into.

Dutch government officials might very well have been correct in their assessment of what had happened to Rockefeller. But they had reasons to present their stated scenario—a plausible one—and then close the book on it. This was 1961; revolutionary demands for independence were sprouting all over the world. In the prior century, European powers were able to justify their colonial holdings by pointing out that they were bringing "civilization" to the unwashed natives. Sure, there was some extraction of native resources here and there, but the natives were getting schooling, rules of law, rail lines, and modern infrastructure in return. Everybody won.

Except only a few won. Now, after World War II, when the Allies won and liberated millions, justifications for imperialism fell flat. Britain accelerated its painful process of dismantling its network of possessions, allowing for self-determination in such disparate places as Burma, India, and Ghana. The Dutch, too, were watching the dwindling of their empire, giving up or loosening control in Indonesia, Suriname, and Curacao. Because New Guinea was just so damned out there, little international attention was paid to the place. Once the Indonesians had established independence, they licked their collective chops over the island, but they weren't yet in much of a position to challenge the Dutch.

With Rockefeller's very, very high-profile disappearance, the eyes of the world were trained, for the first time, on Netherlands New Guinea. Once people got the answer to the question "Where the hell is that?" the next obvious question was: "Why are the Dutch there, and what are they doing?" The lurid tales coming out of New Guinea after Rockefeller's disappearance made one thing clear: that place was anything but "civilized," at least to the thinking of the average Westerner. The Dutch, finally, would have to make an accounting of their presence there. Rockefeller's disappearance threw some seriously unwanted attention on the island.

Wassing clung to the boat for another full day before he was rescued, some forty miles out to sea. His choice to stay—not that he really had a choice—

proved the correct one. Rockefeller, as far as anyone knew, hadn't been seen by plane, boat, or land. Wassing guessed that he never made it as far as shore. "Even if you are only thirty feet from shore, you don't stand a chance against that abnormally heavy tide," he said. And Rockefeller had some five-plus miles to cover.

Perhaps Michael Rockefeller was doomed by a sense of entitlement; after all, he had grown up with a wide and inviolable safety net. Whatever thing he tried, he would have the backing of power, prestige, and influence. In this environment, he could be forgiven for feeling as if misfortune was not something that could touch him personally. But in this case, that supposition was dead wrong.

Nelson Rockefeller and his daughter Mary, Michael's twin sister, made the long trip to New Guinea to aid in the search in whatever way they could. When they (and eventually almost one hundred news reporters from around the world) arrived in the newly appointed search headquarters of Merauke, normally a collection of little more than huts and around three thousand inhabitants, the Dutch authorities greeted them with bad news. The people here are headhunters and cannibals, they noted, perhaps pressing the point a bit as a roundabout explanation for their failures to fully civilize the place. If Michael had made it to shore, what awaited him . . . well, that was better left implied. Maybe it was of some comfort to know that the Dutch naval authorities didn't believe it had even gotten to that point. Rockefeller had to swim five miles against a current. He probably drowned in the sea—a terrible death, yes, but one that at least fit into the natural order of things. His having been eaten, his skull becoming a container from which to smoke—all of it was too much to contemplate.

But a glimmer of what can be described as horrified hope emerged a week after Rockefeller's disappearance. The *Sydney Morning Herald* led with "Rockefeller May be Captive in Dutch N.G. Jungle." The Australian paper arrived at this possibility on the word of a Dutch officer who knew the area and its inhabitants well. He figured that if Rockefeller had made it to shore, he wouldn't have been eaten. (Others seconded this; the notion of a native eating a white man was preposterous. These were people with very refined and specific ideas about death and spirits. No one in these coastal tribes had ever eaten a white person. Doing so now would potentially visit upon them some unprecedented ills. In fact, many missionaries and anthropologists used to move around unarmed because of the natives' fervent belief in this very point.) The Dutch officer suggested, instead, that the tribes would keep Rockefeller out of sight for fear that they would be punished if the Dutch authorities found him in their possession in bad physical shape. They would nurse him back to health before they let anyone know that the white man with all the goods was in a village hut.

Another cultural point can't be underestimated. Rockefeller was rich; his knives, hatchets, and tobacco showed that clearly enough. He was a white man, part of the tribe that seemed to possess the powers of wealth. Holding him would obviously be advantageous to any group; it would only have to make him conjure up those powers of wealth in its presence for everyone to benefit.

But, yes, he was white—and that meant he was also part of the tribe that had visited a massacre upon the village of Otsjanep three years earlier. If this was the village that held him now, that could spell his doom. Rockefeller would provide an easy and convenient opportunity for settling old scores and avenging the as yet unavenged dead.

The accounts of Nelson and Mary Rockefeller's visit vary depending on who's telling them. There was a mixture of disdain and pity for them; when they arrived, it was clear by their stunned reactions as they flew over the 1,400-square-mile search area of swamp and jungle, holding field glasses to their eyes, that they hadn't grasped just how remote this place was in which their loved one had disappeared. So there was the pity, especially for Mary, who gave in to several fits of hysterical sobbing. But many searchers felt their hubris as well—the attitude that of course he would be found. Calamities such as this happen to other people; they don't happen to Rockefellers. But Nelson held daily press briefings in extraordinarily difficult situations and dutifully answered painful questions, only losing his cool once. When, after a week, they finally announced they were going back home, Michael's father met with the press in Hollandia and summed it all up this way: "It was an accident. The boat upset. Michael was never happier than here in Netherlands New Guinea." When he was met by American press back home in New York, Nelson added, "He has always loved people and been loved by them. He had tremendous enthusiasm and drive and loved life and beauty in people, in art, in nature." Nelson Rockefeller, governor of New York and presidential candidate, looked away, in a brief moment when his brave public facade slipped. He whispered, "Things can happen."

The Soviet propaganda newspaper *Pravda* had a field day with the whole affair, suggesting that because of Michael's wealthy upbringing he was predisposed to a bad accident and that his abandonment of Wassing was certainly no surprise. With the Cold War in full swing, this was to be expected. But the Rockefellers met with hostility in unexpected quarters as well. Perhaps it was some unannounced delight in seeing the superrich have to deal with real problems, the sorts of problems that money couldn't fix. The lead reporter for the *South Pacific Post,* an Australian, suggested (and he wouldn't be the only one) that Michael Rockefeller was a simpleton and something of a family embarrassment and that with his father in reelection mode for governor, it would work well to spirit Michael out of the country. Further, showing up and playing the part of the grieving father would do wonders for his sympathy and compassion ratings, enough, even, to offset the effects of a public divorce.

Many Aussies enjoyed the entire spectacle. There was little love for Michael and even less for his father, a man they found extraordinarily stingy after it was learned that the Australian government footed the entire search bill.

But the *New York Times* was sympathetic. Nevertheless, its reporter on the scene, Homer Bigart, wasn't very optimistic about Rockefeller's fate and gave what became the generally accepted view when he wrote, "For as much as twelve miles offshore, the Arafura is tawny with silt and jungle flotsam. Then quite suddenly the water is green and clear. From a low-flying plane one sees schools of sharks . . . and the writhing of poisonous sea serpents, some thirteen feet long." The implication was clear: if Michael Rockefeller didn't drown, a sea creature made a meal of him. Peter Hastings, a respected reporter at the *Australian* and an editor of the journal *New Guinea,* concurred. "I was there during the search," he said. "We flew over the area many times at low altitudes. You have never seen a place so infested with sharks and saltwater crocodiles. It would have been impossible for a man to swim through all that and live. Saltwater crocodiles are particularly vicious."

This, of course, jibed with the official Dutch view. But innuendo and rumor allowed the Rockefeller story to continue; in the absence of bodily evidence, of course, there were other possibilities. (Besides, it's simply erroneous to say that no one could have swum through that water and survived; after all, the two native boys did precisely that.) And one of the people who offered a different view had plenty of credibility. Eight years after Michael Rockefeller's disappearance (and his subsequent disappearance from the front pages), the *New York Post* ran a story with the headline, "Was Rocky's Son Killed By Natives?" Within the article was this: "A Dutch priest [the Reverend Corneles

Van Kessel] . . . said he is certain the son of the governor was slain by natives in retaliation for the killing of four tribesmen by Dutch officials." Van Kessel, sounding very sympathetic to both Rockefeller and the natives, was quoted as saying, "The tribesmen had killed him as revenge for the senseless killing of four of their brothers by some Dutch officials . . . Those men were innocent and they were shot to death for no reason. That was nearly four years earlier, and the tribe never forgot."

Van Kessel, who enjoyed good relations with the coastal Otsjanep tribesmen, claimed that some of them told him that they had, in fact, killed Rockefeller after coming across him swimming for shore. They said that when they found the white man, he was wearing only eyeglasses and underwear, a detail only Wassing could have known at the time of Rockefeller's disappearance. They even said they held his eyeglasses at the village (though no outsider ever saw them). Several of the tribesmen argued against killing Rockefeller, fearing major reprisals from the Dutch patrols. But a fierce chief named Ajam had lost a relative in the Dutch murders in 1958. Ajam decided to kill Rockefeller on the spot, finally settling the lingering, unresolved payback. It had been almost four years, after all, during which the four deceased had been unavenged—a delay that, frankly, a fighting chief such as Ajam should have been ashamed of. One white man, one member of the "Dutch tribe," was enough—it had to be a killing, but not necessarily a number that matched the Otsjanep deceased.

John Ryan, a reporter working at the Australian Broadcasting Company, supported Van Kessel's account. He, too, laid the blame squarely on the Dutch patrol in 1958 and also accused Dutch officials of complicity in covering up the killings for political reasons after Rockefeller's disappearance. "You can bet those Dutch officials had something to do with hushing it up," he said. "A killing like that wouldn't look good on their record at a time they were trying to convince the world that they had successfully pacified the area and were more qualified to administer it than the Indonesians, who were first starting their big drive to take over the territory."

In 1961, a French team released the film *The Sky Above, the Mud Below,* an Oscar-winning documentary filmed mostly in Otsjanep. The film's producer, Gérard Delloye, became Ajam's adopted tribal son. Delloye believed it was not merely possible that Ajam had killed Rockefeller; he thought it was a certainty. "I believe Ajam was Rockefeller's killer," Delloye said. "We of the film crew knew of it long before it was made public, but did not want to be accused of sensationalism or publicity seeking in regard to our film. We were very much aware of the still smoldering resentment of the tribe toward the Dutch over the recent killing of their clansmen." (In a terrifying twist to this part of the story, the French crew had filmed the elaborate carving of a *bis* pole; this could have been for the still-unavenged killings in 1958. Later, when Rockefeller came into the village and bartered over the pole, it may very well have been the pole that would later be discarded once Rockefeller himself became the revenge payback and the pole had served its purpose.)

The story got a further boost from a report later in the *Sydney Morning Herald.* Apparently, an Indonesian medical army officer reported that as he was treating a cholera outbreak in the Asmat region, some of the afflicted admitted to killing Rockefeller, believing that their current ill fortune was the result of some sort of magical retribution. One important fact supports this possibility: whether it was because of political reasons, convenience, fear, or simply oversight, during all the massive search operations, no official search went to Otsjanep village. The Dutch no doubt knew that they would have to fight their way into the reliably hostile Otsjanep territory; surely, they had no stomach for a reprise of the dreadful events of 1958. Evidence might have been gleaned if searchers had visited during that first week after Rockefeller's disappearance.

Aside from its titillating nature, this account also helps to rebut another argument against Rockefeller's having made it to shore—that even if he had managed to evade all the nasty man-eaters inhabiting that water, once he had made shore, the thick tangle of mangrove roots would have blocked his passage to land. Add the feet-thick quicksand mud, and the combination of these two hazards would be enough to do in anyone, especially someone exhausted after a strenuous swim through tough currents. However, according to Van Kessel, tribesmen picked up Rockefeller before he reached the mangroves.

It must have been relief at first. Rockefeller had enjoyed good relations with the natives and a reputation as an honest broker. Despite his exhaustion from the challenging swim, the sight of a canoe splitting the water and making its way assuredly toward him must have allowed Rockefeller to let up, perhaps even smile at his good fortune. He had made it, and all that was left now was a leisurely ride back to shore, where he could secure help for Wassing. Did the relief turn immediately to horror, or was it disbelief, when the fishing spear was raised and came down, piercing the surface of the water first, and then, almost as easily, his skin and organs?

Some version of this is precisely what took place, if the account given by Dutch missionary Father Van Kessel, among others, can be believed. According to his account, villagers—including Ajam—boasted of killing Rockefeller even before the news of the disappearance had spread. They said that they came across him exhausted and panting, and that one of them had taken his fishing spear and stuck Rockefeller. They then had dragged him to shore and finished him off there.

Though reported to the highest authorities, the story got little credence in the Netherlands. It was the old Otsjanep problem again, one that the Dutch surely didn't want to revisit. Van Kessel said that he wrote a report stating his view and that "[Dutch] officials denied it . . . because they were ashamed. They were afraid it would be learned why Michael died." Perhaps this was the reason no one ever visited the village during the search. Perhaps they were frightened as well. The Otsjanep villagers still had lingering resentments toward the Dutch. Whatever the reason, no one in Otsjanep was ever even taken in to the police. One inspector did later ask villagers questions, got several boastful confessions, and dutifully reported them. His report was deleted from the final official version. It was almost as if the killing of Michael Rockefeller and its subsequent cover-up—if indeed it did happen this way— would provide the final severance from the open sore that still bled from the disastrous 1958 patrol.

But what happened need not automatically be seen as so devious—perhaps this was simple tact by the Dutch. Maybe everybody knew what had really happened. Maybe the contemplation of anything other than the official version was simply too much to bear.

Van Kessel's account got little play in America. But in Australia and on the island of New Guinea itself, it became generally accepted that Michael Rockefeller became a main course, roasted on a spit and served with a side of sago.

Perhaps revenge cults, head-hunting, and cannibalism simply make for a better story than simple drowning or death by croc or shark, creatures that we don't find irrational for eating humans. Or maybe, as difficult as it is to admit, people delight in the notion of someone ultrawealthy meeting such an incredible end. But as the *New York Times* put it at the time: "The loss of a son is not easier to bear in a mansion than a cottage."

And, after all, the idea that Rockefeller failed to make it to shore isn't just possible, but perhaps even likely. Yes, the two native boys made it, but they swam for land not long after the boat was swamped; by the time Rockefeller made the attempt, the boat had drifted for miles out to sea.

But those arguing for Rockefeller's having made it were many, and included some pretty credible sources. A Dutch missionary named Gerard Zegwaard suggested a version of events that included Rockefeller's making land. While eating one evening with other priests living up and down the coast, Zegwaard asked these men, whose cumulative experience in the area amounted to more than a century, if they had ever recalled a shark attack on a human. To a man, they said no. Crocodiles were a different story, but in the rare cases when a crocodile became a man-eater, everyone knew about it, and hunting teams went out and killed the beast. Ninety-nine times out of a hundred, a crocodile flees from the sound of an approaching human. Even if a crocodile had gotten Rockefeller, Zegwaard pointed out, it's well known that crocs always drag their victims onto land and kill them there. The corpse sits for days, even weeks, before it's devoured completely. Considering the search of the coast going on in the weeks after Rockefeller disappeared, someone surely would have seen something.

A doctor specializing in tropical medicine, Ary Kemper, supported this view. He had lived in the Asmat for a decade and said, "In all the years here I have never heard of one human being attacked. The natives swim and fish without fear of them. They just don't seem to be man-eaters. Not along this part of the coast. Believe me, I would have learned of any such attack." Despite the fact that Rockefeller would have been swimming against the tide, Kemper said of the young man, "[He] was a powerful swimmer, and with those floats on his back [the empty jerricans] he could not have drowned."

So then Rockefeller was dead, killed and eaten by Otsjanep visitors. Or was he?

In 1968, Milt Machlin, a writer for *Argosy* magazine, was visited in his Manhattan office by an Australian sailor-smuggler named John Donahue. The Tasmanian claimed that he had seen Rockefeller, very much alive, on a remote flyspeck island off the New Guinea mainland, looking very ragged, squinting terribly, and hobbling around on a swollen and badly misshapen knee. "I am Michael Rockefeller," he allegedly said to Donahue. "Can you help me?"

Machlin initially had some trouble believing Donahue's story. But Machlin had enough knowledge about New Guinea from his time in the American Army signal battalion and the New Guinea campaign in World War II to have a good idea whether Donahue was simply making up something to extract a bribe or was engaged in some other nefarious scheme. The two spoke in a Manhattan bar, and it was clear that Donahue knew his stuff. He said that he and two other witnesses—he named them—had seen Rockefeller on the north coast of an island called "Kanapua or Kanaboora—something like that. Hard to tell when you hear it from the natives ... It lies around a hundred and fifty degrees longitude by eight degrees south latitude."

Because he had named verifiable sources and had given such a precise geographic location, Machlin was intrigued. But why hadn't Donahue and his accomplices simply rescued Rockefeller then? "We knew we couldn't even be seen near a harbor within thousands of miles of the area without risking arrest on the murder charges. We would have liked to help the kid, but it was just too chancy." The "murder charges" Donahue referred to stemmed from an earlier incident when he and his companions got into a scuffle with Dutch patrol officers who had tried to board their boat, which was laden with smuggled goods. Donahue and his crew fired on the patrol and wound up killing three people. Now, they felt they couldn't take the risk of traveling with a handicapped white man; however, they did promise Rockefeller that they would send for help as soon as possible.

Donahue, through a circuitous route, wound up in New York on his way to some undisclosed location far from the reach of international law. There, he visited Machlin because he had earlier seen Machlin's story on Rockefeller's disappearance in an edition of *Argosy*. Machlin noted that Donahue didn't ask for money or anything else; this made him less suspicious. Donahue explained his interest in the Rockefeller case this way: "I have been nothing but a criminal all my life. I just thought I would help someone else for once. Besides, I promised the kid."

Machlin was now more than a little curious. He wrote, "If by the remotest flight of fancy Donahue's story should actually be true, Michael Rockefeller would have to be found. And I was determined to be the one to do it."

He set off, investigating the possibility that Rockefeller was, in fact, alive and living on New Guinea, or close by. Machlin made his tortuous way to Kanapu, the little island where Donahue had claimed to have seen Rockefeller, only to find it deserted. There were huts, but no people. If Rockefeller had been held there, he certainly wasn't there anymore. Machlin's 1972 book, *The Search for Michael Rockefeller,* recounts the story. The journey, while providing a good read, didn't produce any more clues as to the fate of Michael Rockefeller.

Nevertheless, Donahue's wasn't the only "Rockefeller sighting." An Australian trader named Roy Hogan claimed that he had seen Rockefeller in the Asmat eight years after his disappearance. Hogan and his two-man crew were taking a break on the banks of the Ewta River when a large group of natives came upon them, apparently startled by Hogan and his crew. They all stopped and looked at one another. Among the native crew was a tall, bespectacled, bearded white man. Hogan began to follow them when they walked away. As he did so, they showed some hostile signs, and Hogan beat it. Rockefeller didn't occur to him until later, back in Port Moresby when he caught a picture of Rockefeller in the papers. He was sure that the man along the river and the man in the paper were one and the same.

This account supports the popular theory that Rockefeller voluntarily melded into the jungle and jungle life to escape the shackles of his name and the expectations that went with it. This is, in a word, absurd. It would require the cover-up and collusion of thousands of tribesmen (many quite hostile to each other) to keep silent to every outsider that passed through, whether Dutch official, American anthropologist, or Australian investigative reporter. It would also require of Rockefeller the voluntary immersion in a downright difficult and frankly unpleasant life. It's one thing to admire a "pure" culture from afar, or to delve into it for months, even years. Investigative reporter John Godwin described the Asmat Coast as "a tangled morass of bog and forest, thick with insects and leeches but unmarred by a single road, airfield, or telephone wire. Most of the villages lay so deeply buried in the jungle that their people rarely saw the sun." This is the place to which Rockefeller sought to escape?

Eventually the pull of cold beer, air-conditioning, or soft beds would probably be too much—and if not these creature comforts, at least a wish to be rid of the crushing heat and humidity, thick forest canopy, constant rot, and relentless mosquitoes.

For the rest of Nelson Rockefeller's life, he actively worked to prevent further searches and investigations, feeling the matter sadly closed and wanting the thing to be done, not to linger ad nauseam in salacious implication. But when he died on January 26, 1979, his ex-wife, Michael's mother, Mary Rockefeller, contacted Australian private investigator Frank Monte and asked him to head back to New Guinea, to the area by now called Irian Jaya, to see if any lingering

rumors of Michael's being held captive in the jungles panned out. Monte
was offered $50,000 for the job. His account of his investigation reads like
Apocalypse Now meets *Fear and Loathing on New Guinea*. He eventually bought
three skulls—belonging to the only three white men allegedly ever killed in the
village—from some Asmat warriors, paying one outboard motor for them. He
dutifully delivered these to Mary Rockefeller and never heard from her again.
It's doubtful any of these skulls was Rockefeller's.

The Asmat tribesmen, though told by government officials and missionaries
that their belief system made them absolute savages, surely weren't stupid. Of
course they offered "Rockefeller's skull." They got a pretty price for it. This
white dude's skull was worth a hell of a lot. No wonder then that "Rockefeller's
skull" kept turning up, offered to every trader, investigator, and government
official for years to come.

Michael Rockefeller could be called, rather simply, a victim of bad timing and
placement. Without his full understanding, he had descended into a cultural,
geographical, and political hornet's nest. On a macro level, New Guinea
was a land at war with itself and tugged and pushed by foreign powers that
didn't have natives' best interests in mind. The disappearance of the son of a
presidential candidate and billionaire in a land that the Dutch government
was "civilizing" would reflect unfavorably on the Dutch arguments about
continued control over the island being made at that very moment at the
United Nations. The spectacle of Rockefeller going missing—and the added
horror of the possibility of his being cannibalized—made Dutch claims to
the land even more tenuous. Dutch officials had warned Rockefeller that his
well-known desire for skulls "was creating a demand which could not be met
without bloodshed." So much of what was going wrong there, the argument
went, was his fault. However, the very fact that much was going wrong there
directly contradicted Dutch claims that they had successfully brought the
savages into the twentieth century and away from their Stone Age ways. Soon
after Rockefeller's disappearance, the Netherlands would give up trying. Within
two years, Netherlands New Guinea would be given to the Indonesians and
renamed West Irian; its old capital, Hollandia, was renamed Jayapura.

As a microcosm of his poor timing and placement, Michael's near-
landfall—if, indeed, it did happen that way—in the waters outside Otsjanep

was an incredible stroke of bad luck. This was a hostile village bent on revenge. Had he washed up just a mile or two away to either side along the coast, his chances for rescue would have been rather decent.

Ironically, Rockefeller's disappearance while hunting Asmat art created a demand for it among wealthy collectors from Europe and North America. Even today, they swoop into New Guinea and meet with the "untouched" tribes that await their arrival. The tribesmen, decked out in native finery to make the experience more authentic, trot out hastily made carvings that fetch great prices. The pieces—totems, canoe paddles, storyboards—then hang in Upper East Side apartments, where they undoubtedly make for great party chatter about that trip to New Guinea to see the noble savages.

As for Rockefeller's acquisitions, they remain on display today in the Metropolitan Museum of Art's Michael C. Rockefeller Wing.

7/ A Fine Kind of Madness:
Johnny Waterman

We Americans have become far removed from the defenses that could save us in natural extremes. We don't possess the lung expansion of Nepalese Sherpas, who can often withstand heights of twenty thousand–plus feet without supplemental oxygen. We don't have the ability of Australian Aborigines to sleep naked on the ground in forty-degree temperatures, falling into something like catatonia until the warmth of a new day sets them moving again.

But this is not to say that we're wholly unprepared. The human body is an extraordinary machine. If you're lost and making your way through deep snow on a viciously cold day (let's say, minus thirty degrees Fahrenheit), initially your core body temperature will be near or above one hundred degrees. The energy required to trudge through the white stuff makes you feel comfortable. Hell, aside from the bits of exposed flesh—maybe your face and slits of skin peeping from between your sleeves and your gloves—you feel downright warm.

But at some point you stop—to orient or reorient, maybe to realize, to your horror, that you've come the wrong way. Now what do you do? Retrace your steps, *undo* all the effort you've undertaken to get to this point? No, it's better to keep going. But that could take you farther in the wrong direction. So you stop. You stand and you weigh your options. But the more you stay still, the colder you get. The sweat you worked up getting here is now a killer—a thin layer of moisture that's freezing on your skin. You start to shiver violently. Simple mechanics become increasingly impossible. A fire? With those freezing fingers? Those fingers, now exposed in the effort of lighting some wood, that tremble even more, deaden, turn dark blue, then black?

It is said that the very end of the line when freezing to death can actually be one of the more pleasant ways to die. You're no longer cold, all is numb, and you peacefully—without protest—give in. If this was your plan all along, what sweet welcome you must give those final moments.

But what if this was not your plan? What if you've been plowed under by an avalanche, a giant slab falling and shuttling and picking up speed and bulldozing everything in its path with hundreds of tons of pressure? A human body, of course, is no match. Better if it kills you right off. If not, it manages to leave you unmercifully alive within its grasp, snow packed in your ears, eyes, and mouth. When it stops moving above you, it reveals the most horrifying thing a human can face; it's the thing Edgar Allan Poe wrote about in "The Premature Burial," the title needing no further explication.

Though you are buried in snow, it's not the cold that's the problem. It's the dark, the density, the pressure. If you've been lucky enough to have a space in front of your mouth, there's a pocket where you can breathe oxygen—after all, the snow is loaded with the stuff. But here's the rub: the more you breathe in and subsequently exhale, the more the condensation from your breath will form a hard shell of ice on that pocket. Once the pocket is sealed, the oxygen is gone. More cannot get through, and then it's a quick end.

Johnny Waterman was born in 1952, the second of three boys to Guy and Emily Waterman. From all familial accounts, John was toughness and frustration from the start. He would be inconsolable if his Lincoln Logs collapsed, almost unmovable despite his pint-size frame.

His father, Guy Waterman, came from privilege, a product of two wealthy and well-connected Connecticut families. Guy Waterman's father taught physics at Yale and later became the first president of the National Science Foundation. Guy lived his childhood on a wooded, 10-acre farm in North Haven and spent innumerable hours tramping gleefully through the forests. When the family moved to Cambridge, Massachusetts, Guy was crushed—in his estimation, he was never fully suited for city life. Despite his placement in privileged schooling at the Taft School in Connecticut, Guy fell in with the masses who couldn't be found in such elite company. His friends were black or from the working classes. After the family moved to Washington, D.C., Guy became increasingly rebellious, drinking and smoking and haunting all-night jazz clubs, where he enjoyed a well-earned reputation as an ace pianist. He was good enough to eventually make his living with a ragtime band, the Riverboat Trio.

Mount McKinley

Eventually, his rebellion became too much for his parents, who committed him to a lockup in George Washington Hospital's psychiatric ward. As part of his further rebellion, he married at eighteen and had kids rather quickly afterward. Perhaps it was a result of his forced move from a place he loved to a school he loathed leading to his active revolt against his parents, but Waterman was infected with some bug that assured that moments of happiness would always be followed by gnawing resentment toward the world and his place within it. Johnny Waterman, and to a different degree his brother Bill, would inherent this same tendency. But while father and sons shared a volatility in mood and an inclination toward nadirs of depression, they were separated by a generation. Accordingly, the three tried to calm their respective demons with drugs. For the father, it was alcohol; for the boys, it was weed and hallucinogens. The alcohol, not surprisingly, fueled an even further downward spiral.

Guy Waterman became alienated from wife, coworkers, musicians—and his sons. He even contemplated suicide. But he was no easily broken man; after reading the classic mountaineering book *The Climb Up to Hell*, he managed to cast off all that was destroying him in favor of mountain climbing, something that focused his energy into a healthy pursuit and brought reconciliation with his children.

The book, published in 1962 and written by Jack Olsen, chronicles the ill-fated 1957 expedition in the Swiss Alps that claimed the lives of three men. The lone survivor was saved only by a hastily organized rescue operation featuring dozens of Europe's finest climbers. The story is amazing, and the book is expertly written. It has sunk its claws into many readers, and Waterman was no exception. Indeed, he was transfixed by it. It took him back first in spirit and then in reality to the woods of his New England childhood. Waterman joined the Appalachian Mountain Club's New York chapter, and he learned how to rock climb upstate.

He passed on his passion for the sport to his sons. Johnny, especially, inherited his father's zeal for climbing. He also internalized his father's particular climbing ethic, involving as little dependence on gear as possible. While a man should be safe, sensible, and steady, the adventure should, in the end, be about just him and his rock—kind of a reverse Sisyphus: man in control of his rock instead of the other way around. Johnny soon showed an aptitude that far outshone even his father's.

Guy described his son's actions on the rocks as an explosion of power: "He was not beauty, he was energy. He was not control, he was uncontrolled joy." Guy echoed this sentiment later in a letter to writer and climber Jon Waterman (no relation): "What I recall of Johnny was an explosive energy and ferocious ecstasy on the rock or ice—a masterfully competent but electric, volcanic, creative vitality." Johnny's moves on the rock appeared purely instinctive and absolute. Where his foot fell, there was a hold. Where his hand landed, there was a sliver. The rock seemed to bend itself to Johnny's outsize will. He was pure artistry on his climbs, moving his diminutive body up and down with sure-footedness. He earned the nickname "Super Squirrel."

Johnny's training regimen has been well-documented: walking home from school more than two miles as quickly as possible, touching the door, and turning around to do it again. Doing four hundred push-ups a day. As with his father, nothing for Johnny Waterman was ever half-assed. Climbing claimed his full attention and passion. While still in high school, he pioneered a difficult route on Cannon Mountain in New Hampshire, calling it Consolation Prize. He taught classes on climbing, and while just a teenager, Johnny often led climbing parties during which he wowed even older, accomplished climbers. His enthusiasm was unmistakable, and infectious. If one wasn't too taken aback by his unbridled fervor, then that person would be the beneficiary of a limitless store of encouragement. Countless climbers who experienced the "Johnny Waterman treatment" when he was at his best remember that they often accomplished moves one or two skill levels beyond what they thought they were capable of completing.

The climbing proved to be a point of shared joy between father and sons and served to bridge the gap that had previously widened between them. In the summer of 1966, Guy, Johnny, and Bill, along with their dog, climbed all forty-six known four-thousand-footers in the White Mountains (two more mountains have been determined to be more than four thousand feet tall since that time). A year and a half later, Guy and Johnny returned to New Hampshire in the winter, a trip that sorely tested their limits. They endured howling storms, temperatures twenty and thirty degrees below zero, winds that topped one hundred miles per hour. The trip nearly killed them—and it was the best thing they had done to that point. For Guy, it confirmed the value in testing oneself against the elements. For Johnny, it was the final reminder—if he needed one—that mountains and climbing would loom over everything in his life.

At age sixteen, Johnny climbed Alaska's Mount McKinley (Denali), North America's highest point at 20,320 feet, making him the third-youngest person ever to do so. After high school, he went to Europe to do more climbing. He went as far east as Turkey, then looped back, climbing through the Alps and making his way to the United Kingdom. His love for the mountains intensified, but it also brought into sharper relief that painful separation between all that he loved in climbing and, essentially, all of everything else. He once wrote of the "barriers in my mind toward meeting other people and relaxing, the barriers that only let down when I'm alone in my 'home' in the mountains." While he excelled in mountains, Johnny Waterman fell woefully short in social situations. Desperately wanting a girlfriend, but unable to perfect the social requirements necessary for obtaining one, Waterman became obsessed with the things that he saw as lacking in his life. He once wrote to his father, "As far as John the climber goes, I've already defined my lines. It's John the rest of the time that needs to be found now." Though it's not unusual for a nineteen-year-old to feel this way, he would maintain the sentiment for the rest of his life.

This "mountain loneliness" he referred to showed up even when he wasn't alone on the mountain. More and more, Johnny's enthusiasm became too difficult for others to endure. It manifested itself in wild bursts of anger and frustration when things didn't go exactly as planned. While he rarely directed that anger at another person, Waterman would sometimes rant about something as simple as a rip in a pair of pants. Climbing partners took note of the fact that his quick climbs toward summits often pushed the limits of safety.

He seemed to lack prudence and due caution, but was such an expert climber that he almost always managed to keep himself out of any real danger. But for someone without his natural expertise, the frenetic pace was often too much to take. Suggesting a slower approach was enough to invite wrath.

The pejorative term is "Little Man's Syndrome," a need for the undersized man to constantly prove himself, to the grand irritation of all around him—much like a relentless terrier that won't stop yapping, sinks its teeth into your ankles, and won't let go. Johnny was five foot three on a stretch, and while he developed good muscle tone as a result of climbing, he was sinewy and wiry, not at all bulky. In this, he was similar to his father, Guy. But like many men with a smallish physical stature, the Watermans compensated in other ways, and their displays of prowess and competence earned them the respect of many around them.

While his personal life was falling apart, Guy Waterman's professional life was certainly stable. He enjoyed a career as a speechwriter on Capitol Hill, working for Presidents Eisenhower, Nixon, and Ford, among others. He eventually parlayed that job into one as a corporate speechwriter at General Electric in New York. But professional stability and rock climbing weren't enough to save Guy Waterman's strained marriage, which finally fell apart when Johnny was still a teenager. But far from devastating, the period following the divorce was incredibly rewarding, for Guy at least. The divorce freed him to pursue even more climbing. When he met a fellow climber named Laura Johnson, then working at the newly founded *Backpacker* magazine, in 1969 at the Shawangunks in New York—perhaps the best climbing spot east of the Rocky Mountains—the two hit it off, and Guy soon remarried.

Guy and Laura shared the same environmental ethic and the same passion for climbing. Together, they fell in love with the ethos espoused within Helen and Scott Nearing's book *Living the Good Life*. The book is essentially a primer on how to chuck the modern world and its complications and make a go of it off the grid, deep in the woods somewhere. The book's subtitle, "How to Live Sanely and Simply in a Troubled World," proved an irresistible notion. The Watermans did just that, leaving their jobs, moving to a remote location in Vermont on thirty-nine acres, building a rustic cabin without electricity or plumbing, and growing all their own food. They called the place Barra, after the Scottish island that was once home to Waterman's ancestors. Together, the two of them would write a series of well-regarded and successful books (*Backwoods Ethics: A Guide to Low-Impact Camping and Hiking; Forest and Crag: A History of Hiking, Trail Blazing, and Adventure in the Northeast Mountains; Wilderness Ethics: Preserving the Spirit of Wildness;* and *A Fine Kind of Madness: Mountain Adventures Tall and True*). *Forest and Crag,* published in 1989, was dedicated to Johnny Waterman and came in at nearly a thousand pages. It remains the seminal work on the history of recreation in the Northeast.

The couple enjoyed mythic status as the environmental conscience of the White Mountains. They adopted a section of the Appalachian Trail (accepting responsibility for maintaining it), continued to write and live their conservation ethos, and eventually climbed every four-thousand-foot peak in the mountains no fewer than seven times each (sixteen for Guy, hitting every mountain from all four directions).

The silent demons that had haunted Guy Waterman all his life certainly didn't disappear; however, with few interactions save with his wife, they were less apt to be brought to the fore by some repulsive societal interaction and thus much easier to abate. But being so far off the grid did create distance, both literal and metaphorical, from his sons. Johnny especially found the severance of his parents' relationship and the subsequent removal of his father from society to be an especially difficult bridge to cross, even though Johnny was getting older and living independently.

Johnny's love of mountains made Alaska an obvious attraction for settlement, but several people familiar with the Waterman family saga have noted that Johnny's move to Alaska after his father had taken up residence in the Vermont woods meant that the son—subconsciously or no—was almost as far away as possible while still being on the same continent. Intentionally or not, Johnny's move west marked a period of estrangement between father and son. Bill would eventually move out west as well. Each son only made one trip to Barra. The painful distance from his father that had tormented Guy Waterman was now repeating itself with his own sons.

Johnny, meanwhile, continued to try to find solace in climbing. But Bill became increasingly dependent on drugs, and his life took a turn that he never really recovered from when one of his legs was destroyed. He had been dozing in a freight yard, waiting for his opportunity to hop one of the trains, when an attachment bump sent a car rolling over his leg. In May 1973, at the age of twenty-two, Bill wrote a cryptic letter to his father, telling him that he was "Going off on a trip. Not in Alaska. Will be in touch when I get back." Where he was headed, he didn't say. That would be the last time anyone ever heard from him. Bill's disappearance marked a sad end to a man who had so much potential. Prior to losing his leg to a train, his brain to drugs, and then, most probably, his life to some vague notion of going off somewhere, Bill had been a National Merit Scholar headed for a bright future. While Guy Waterman maintained for years that his son had probably melted into an Athapaskan Eskimo village up north, those who spent time with Bill in his last years had no doubt that he walked off to commit suicide—how and where were the only real mysteries.

So his brother had disappeared, probably died. This had a great effect on Johnny. And it certainly wouldn't be the last death he would have to endure. Boyd Everett, an important mountaineer who had gained fame for first ascents all over Alaska, was an early climbing partner of Johnny's, seeing the extraordinary skill in the young Waterman. While his father, Guy, had been the most important figure in Johnny's early New England climbing experience, Everett became something of a mentor in Johnny's alpine climbing. But Everett and six other climbers were killed in an avalanche in Nepal. The deaths had a big impact on the young and emotional Waterman. Not long after, two more of Waterman's climbing partners from expeditions in Alaska and Canada died as well, this time on the Matterhorn in Switzerland. Eventually, no fewer than nine of Johnny Waterman's onetime climbing partners died, all but one of them in climbing accidents.

Climbing was supposed to be the anodyne. Now, Johnny Waterman was caught in a vicious cycle: climb to heal the pain, climb to be reminded, tormented every agonizing step of the way that his one true love was a killer. He once described climbing as a "deeply tragic affair."

And that affair was becoming more and more single-minded. His obsession: Mount Hunter.

Hunter's Athapaskan name is Begguya, meaning the "child of Denali," and many people regard the mountain as the most difficult fourteen-thousand-footer in North America. Mount Hunter sits in the Alaska Range and tops out at more than fourteen thousand five hundred feet. While this height can be relatively modest in mountaineering terms, the conditions on Hunter can make climbing the mountain almost suicidal. Writer and climber Glenn Randall wrote of the some of the obstacles: "Cornices as airy as meringue [jut] over voids a mile deep. The vertical ice walls [are] as crumbly as a bucket of ice cubes half-thawed then refrozen."

With three other climbers, Waterman had attempted to climb Mount Hunter in 1973. The foursome made it (or so they thought), but Waterman's partners did notice that while he still possessed the same intensity and focus of earlier expeditions, his behavior had become erratic. He was given to fits of uncontrolled cursing and singing strange songs to himself as they climbed. When they did reach what they thought was the summit, they did so in a raging storm. It was only later, down the mountain, that the men realized that in fact they had come a few hundred feet shy of the summit. For Waterman, this meant the entire enterprise had been a failure. It also reinforced his growing sense that mountains were animate beings that were in constant judgment of his piddling efforts. In this case, the mountain had won.

The next year, in a party of five climbers, Waterman climbed the east ridge of 12,240-foot Mount Huntington, also in Alaska. It's an extremely difficult ascent, and the party had great reason to celebrate the feat. But as the four other climbers engaged in congratulations on the summit, they couldn't help but notice that Waterman stood away from the group, staring wistfully at the peak of nearby Mount Hunter.

While that peak had bested him once, Waterman was determined to have the last laugh; he would do Hunter again, this time with a drive and determination that would win him instant fame in mountaineering circles. However, as committed as he was to go back and conquer Hunter, Waterman was becoming increasingly aware of his perhaps unhealthy relationship to climbing and mountains in general. In a letter to a friend, he conceded that he thought there might be something wrong with himself, "mentally." He wrote, "If I continue to climb at such a high degree of intensity I won't live a year or more. I'll either fall somewhere or 'flip out,' either of which will result in the removal of myself from this earth (death)."

Despite these misgivings, Waterman made up his mind to climb Hunter solo. The southeast spur, Waterman's chosen route, had been previously unclimbed, making his ascent a first where teams of climbers had previously failed. If he pulled it off, then he would join the pantheon, that elite group of mountaineers who had done something truly monumental. And in the latter part of the twentieth century, such an accomplishment was getting more and more difficult to lay claim to. The climb had been labeled by some as insane, others as suicidal, and no one would have been surprised if he had died doing it.

His training regimen was intense, and a bit bizarre, involving, among other eccentricities, submerging himself in bathtubs full of ice cubes. But it paid off. It took Waterman nearly three months to climb Hunter and another nine weeks to descend, but he did it.

Waterman's account of his Hunter solo expedition appeared in the 1978 *American Alpine Journal* (*AAJ*), the annual publication of the American Alpine Club. Founded in 1902, the club "is the leading national organization in the United States devoted to mountaineering, climbing, and the multitude of issues facing climbers." It's America's seminal climbing organization, and its annual journal presents a compendium of daring climbs the world over. Waterman's climb, appearing in the journal as "Mount Hunter Traversed Solo," is more or less a straightforward account. It would, of course, be impossible to adequately capture the magnitude of Waterman's accomplishment in the three and a half pages of text dedicated to his climb. But the journal operated this way, filling its pages with technical jargon read and understood by other climbers, as opposed to mass-market accounts of climbing, say, Everest. In fact, while Waterman's climb easily represented the greatest feat covered in that year's journal, the story is found on page 91, sandwiched between "Huntington's Southeast Spur," by Angus Thuermer, and "Mount Hunter's Southwest Ridge," by Shari Kearney, with nothing to indicate its status as something looming over all other accounts in the book, many of them describing very impressive endeavors nonetheless.

Because Waterman made the trip solo, he had to haul all his own gear, a substantial load, to get him up and down and through the very long period he would spend on the mountain. Waterman had previously gained fame for his light, "alpine" style, as opposed to the "expedition" style favored by many English teams. Expedition-style ascents are easy to define—an expedition involves a slew of people: porters, guides, coolies, Sherpas. Over the years, these teams were trimmed to smaller numbers, while European climbers carried their own gear. Nevertheless, climbers still went in groups of three, four, five people. But Waterman was attempting Hunter expedition-style by himself. This meant that he would have to climb, fix ropes, rappel down, gather his gear, and haul it back up bit by bit. It meant, in the end, that he climbed Hunter the equivalent of twelve times. It was a painstaking and excruciating process, enough to drive anyone completely out of his mind. It's a testament to both Waterman's singular will and his instability that he actually pulled it off.

It takes close inspection of the "Summary of Statistics" at the *AAJ* entry's conclusion to fully realize the magnitude of what Waterman accomplished. The numbers and tallies are impressive enough: *New Route:* Mount Hunter, 14,573 feet. North Summit reached July 26, 1978 (145-day expedition); *Technical Data:* 3,600 feet of rope, 40 ice pitons, pickets, and flukes, 20 rock anchors; *Personnel:* John Waterman.

One lonely name. This climb, the duration of it, surely would have tested any team, even two people, who at least would have had the benefit of keeping each other sane during the more harrowing hours. But there, under "Personnel," we see one solitary person.

As for the expedition's technical aspects, Waterman includes the following:

> *My plans called for a complete solo traverse of the mountain south-to-north and descent of a route on the north side to a fly-out from the north fork of the Tokositna Glacier . . . I would do this route in the most expedition-like style, ferrying my entire 600-pound Base Camp of reserve equipment up each section of the mountain. By re-using my rope as I went along, pulling it up again and again after I had moved supplies up each section, I could climb a route requiring 12,000 feet of rope with only 3,600 feet. To complete the traverse, there were twelve camps. I took an average of twelve round trips on each section, to shuttle gear, though only ten on the descent. My earlier plans to take from 80 to 100 days proved completely inaccurate.*

Waterman's account follows the conventions of the journal. Its descriptions are straightforward and lack the flash and quick wit that can be seen in Waterman's letters to friends. What else is missing is what friends would come to understand later as the absolute anguish he went through in completing his traverse. For example, he writes of the last section of a steep, corniced buttress, "The ropes became frozen and Jumars [a braking and sliding system used to ascend ropes] worked only after considerable thawing with my exhaled breath." What he doesn't write is that the "exhalations" he refers to came at the expense of making himself completely light-headed, and often didn't even work. In those cases, he had to chip away the ice on the Jumars with his ice hammer; the obvious result could have been malfunction of the Jumars, and that could have easily led to equipment failure, and death.

Of the loneliness, he writes only, "On April 19, I received my last flight from Cliff [Hudson, a pilot who periodically dropped food], who flew out some unnecessary rock pitons since I was above the rock now. I wasn't to see another human being for a hundred days." More sardonically: "I noticed I was infested with lice. It was some comfort to know at least I was not alone."

There are vague references to "gloomy feelings" and a mood that was "hardly improved." But he comes nowhere near expressing the utter torment he suffered for long periods. In fact, while he would freely tell anyone who would later listen of his nights of sobbing, his howling into the never-ending winds, his frozen fingers, and his barely endurable loneliness, in the journal he kept it mostly technical and adopted an understated reserve. In fact, he begins one paragraph with the line, "The less said about my carries on this last section the better." The reason, of course, was that it would hardly be suitable in the *American Alpine Journal* to write that the climb during this last section almost broke him. As for the wind that he would later admit nearly drove him to complete madness, he wrote only, "I set up my tent on what was surely the windiest spot on earth." This from a man who had climbed New Hampshire's Mount Washington, which really is the windiest place on earth.

After reaching the summit, he radioed for another food drop, stating, "I'm standing alone on the summit of Mount Hunter after a one hundred twenty-four-day climb of the central buttress. I'm a mighty tired man." Waterman ended his *AAJ* entry this way: "I used my completely sunburned upper torso as an excuse for not load carrying and went to the south summit on July 2, day 101. At 1:50 P.M., I walked onto the broad summit. Who would have known that it would take me another forty-three days to reach my fly-out site." The understatement here is nothing short of extraordinary. After more than one hundred days and nights in such an inhospitable environment, the man couldn't simply call for a helicopter and shuttle home to a warm bath and hot meal. Instead, it would be another month and a half before he could have anything resembling comfort.

Worse, the summit, though the literal pinnacle of all he had poured himself into, was no Eden. There, he fell into a crevasse, endured whiteouts, and stepped out of his crampons no fewer than three times.

It's not at all unusual or unreasonable that Waterman would anthropomorphize Mount Hunter. After all, five months by oneself is enough to drive anyone to inventing companions, and Waterman was a garrulous person who enjoyed and desired the company of others. But Waterman's naming of the portions of mountain around him held ominous overtones: "First Judge," "Second Judge," "Third Judge," and "Little Prince." While this last one sounds relatively benign (perhaps even a hopeful reflection of himself), a prince is still someone who must sit in judgment of subjects. Yes, Waterman's mountain was alive. And clearly it was judging his every move. Indeed, he began his *AAJ* entry describing his "vendetta" against Hunter. Mountains killed people; he knew this for sure, having lost so many friends to mountain accidents and even hearing of the deaths of two climbers on nearby Mount Foraker during his climb on Hunter. Surely Hunter would take his life, too. But when it didn't, when he lived through the terrible ordeal, that, it turned out, was the hardest thing to accept.

While he didn't relate any of this in his *AAJ* entry, he did confide to his journal, "I cried a lot." Now, after finishing the ascent and staring down at the long road home, he had another reason to cry: he was still alive.

In an interview with Glenn Randall, Waterman said: "Something far more precious would be lost if I lived through it than if I died. Living through it would mean that nature wasn't as raw as everybody wanted to believe it was, that man was far superior to the Arctic, far more capable than he had otherwise thought. *Living through it would mean that Hunter wasn't the mountain I thought it was. It was a lot less*" (author's emphasis). These were the questions he was asking himself: How was it that he had actually managed to get the best of one the toughest mountains there was? Was he worthy of that, when so many he knew had succumbed?

But survive he did, saddened now by an ingrained belief in the mountain's loss of stature. He became afflicted with "Hunter madness." Whatever kind of madness it was, his friends and acquaintances couldn't help but see that Waterman had become increasingly unhinged. He often took to prancing around Fairbanks wearing a cape and oversize sunglasses with a big star stuck on the nose bridge, strumming an out-of-tune guitar and serenading passersby. For people slightly off-center, Fairbanks, Alaska, is a pretty decent place to end up. It's far from anywhere and very tolerant of outsize personalities. But even there, Johnny Waterman stood out.

During slide-show presentations of his Hunter climb, he would offer embarrassingly private anecdotes about the climb, such as descriptions of his masturbatory exploits. Audiences didn't know whether to laugh or squirm. Most probably reacted with some combination of both.

It's not wrong to say that for someone to do what Johnny Waterman did on Mount Hunter, he would have to be mad. A sane man couldn't have endured it. But on the other hand, it takes extraordinary steadiness and singularity of will to accomplish what Waterman did. It was, in short, one of the most audacious climbs anyone had ever recorded. But because people increasingly saw Waterman as simply nuts, he lost much of the credit he deserved for the climb. And while there was no shortage of crowds eager to hear his exploits, the Hunter climb did nothing to improve his social or financial prospects. After his solo climb of Hunter, Waterman found himself back in Fairbanks, washing dishes, living on food stamps, and without a girlfriend.

Perhaps victims of solitary confinement could relate, but for most of us, it's impossible to conceive of the crushing aloneness Waterman suffered on Hunter. He endured 145 days in one of the most hostile environments on the planet. Vicious, freezing wind. Whiteouts. Numbing cold.

Hunter changed him. Yes, he had to have been somewhat crazed to have pulled it off. But when he came off that mountain, he was certifiable.

Johnny Waterman turned to politics, running for the Fairbanks North Star Borough school board. He ran on the platform of drug legalization and free sex for the student body. While he unsurprisingly lost (he did manage to receive almost 1,600 votes out of slightly fewer than 9,000 cast), he turned his sights higher: the presidency. He declared his candidacy as a member of the Feed-the-Starving Party. He used his climbing celebrity to call attention to his campaign; he would climb McKinley again, this time in the dead of winter on the mountain's steepest face, and he would bring very little food with him to make a point about the wastefulness of our consumer society. This, if he pulled it off, would surpass his exploits on Hunter. Denali had first been climbed in winter only a decade earlier, and then by an eight-member team. Of the eight, only three made it to the summit, and one died.

On December 20, 1979, Waterman was flown to the Kahiltna Glacier to begin his assault. Within two weeks, faced with the prospect of being alone for a period of time equal to what he had spent on Hunter, Waterman asked to be taken home, saying, "I don't want to die."

Back home, an accidental fire burned down his cabin while he was at work; he lost everything that mattered to him. Aside from climbing equipment, he lost the journals that he had been meticulously keeping, recording the minutia of his daily life. After Hunter, friends noticed that he became obsessed with recording things, often pulling out a pad of paper and pencil to mark casual meetings in the street, logging the duration, company, and content of the conversation. He also wrote reams of poetry in those journals, and he didn't take their destruction very well. It was as if he had lost his very self in that fire. And if he hadn't lost his mind before, this was the point at which friends say he finally went over the edge. None of this was lost on Waterman either.

He took the initiative to call the Alaska Psychiatric Institute in Anchorage, begging them to come get him. He was diagnosed with schizoaffective disorder, marked by prolonged periods of major depressive or manic episodes. The disorder was progressive, meaning it would only get worse. Johnny was still taking street drugs, still obsessing about the mountains. The influence of either—and certainly both—would be too much for anyone with such a condition. He spent two weeks in the institution before checking himself out, complaining that the staff was concerned only with stripping him of all his rights.

In his brief time at the institute, while he tried to get his head together, Johnny Waterman could look out the window in his room. And there, looming in the distance, sat Denali.

The next winter, Waterman renewed his intent to climb Denali solo. In December 1980, he applied for a permit to do so, using "Lone Wolf" as his expedition name.

Waterman's new planned traverse of Denali can only be described as insane: not only would he do it in winter, solo, but he also would begin his trek from the sea, Cook Inlet, more than sixty miles from the Ruth Glacier and the mountain itself. But this attempt was aborted as well, with the change of plans blamed on a failed stove and the extreme cold. He simply couldn't handle the prospect of such cold temperatures night after night, day after day.

But the dream wasn't dead. Two months later, he was at it again. This time, he would not come back down off that mountain.

He finally set off in the spring, carrying very little, and what he did carry constituted woeful underpreparation. In fact, as he socialized with other climbers at the Sheldon Mountain House at six thousand feet, he returned a hand radio to the man who ferried in his supplies, telling him, "I won't be needing this anymore." In case of some emergency when he was all alone on that mountain, a radio would be his only lifeline, his only hope.

He was last seen April 1, 1981, as he headed into a maze of ice and snow pocked with dangerous crevasses on Denali's Ruth Glacier. His route took him to the northwest fork of the glacier, a section that remains unclimbed today because of its propensity for sudden and numerous avalanches. Reinhold Messner, widely considered one of the greatest alpinist mountaineers in the history of the sport, once rejected the crevasse field of Denali's Ruth Glacier as simply too dangerous to attempt. This was where Waterman was headed, with a minimum of gear strapped to a sled, cutting a straight line into a route that demanded constant zigzagging and replotting.

Not surprisingly, he disappeared. But what allows for the mystery and provides fodder for the theorists is that no trace of him was ever found. The only clue as to his final end was not much of a clue after all—a note that read: "3-13-81. 1:42 P.M. My last kiss." The note was found in the Mountain House, scrawled on a cardboard box containing bits of Johnny Waterman's meager cache of gear.

On April 21, Guy and Laura Waterman were busy with the usual demands at Barra when a late-afternoon knock came on the door. The sense of foreboding was immediate; while the Watermans had always hosted friends, arrangements were made weeks, sometimes months in advance. An unannounced visitor didn't portend good things.

Sure enough, the message was that Guy should come to town. The National Park Service in Alaska wanted to talk to him. Guy hurried to East Corinth, Vermont, and made the call; Johnny was missing.

The Park Service's search and rescue efforts for "Lone Wolf" began two weeks after Waterman was last seen on the glacier. By then, it was clear that finding his body would be more probably a result of future chance than of any current organized search effort. In the American Alpine Club's 1982 edition of *Accidents in North American Mountaineering,* the Park Service noted that all that was left that could lead to Waterman (presumably) was a "single set of tracks that were either ski tracks or those left by someone pulling a sled." A day after the Watermans back in Barra were told that Johnny was missing, a private search party circled the Ruth Glacier in a helicopter in good weather. From the air, they could make out a small campsite amid a minefield of crevasses, and there, almost imperceptibly, they could see the "ski or sled tracks" referred to in the incident report. According to a ranger on the search, "We could see the tracks going into the campsite, but none coming out."

In perhaps a perfect encapsulation of the schizophrenic nature of how people received Johnny Waterman—his feats and his limitations—*Outside* magazine once hailed his ascent of Hunter as one of the 1970s' "Ten Greatest Feats"; his disappearance on Denali earned him a place among the same edition's "Ten Strangest Feats."

But people in the climbing community were not quite ready to give up on the mountain genius just yet. A last search, which included one of Johnny's old climbing partners, took a final extensive look for four days. It found nothing.

Had Johnny fooled everyone and disappeared, making a new life for himself somewhere far from the glare of social expectation? One person, Doug Buchanan, thinks yes. Buchanan, a climber from Fairbanks who knew Waterman well, thought Johnny far too expert in the mountains to have died there. Instead, Buchanan contends, he used the mountain as an easy escape, tricking everyone and heading elsewhere, perhaps far from mountains, to start a new life. Buchanan claims that Waterman had once contacted a lawyer in Fairbanks to ask about the consequences of intentionally going missing. It must be remembered that such an act wouldn't have been foreign to Johnny Waterman. As far as he knew, his own brother had pulled it off. Perhaps they even planned it together and met up somewhere, reuniting in a place that offered the promise of peace of mind. Waterman once described growing up in America as "a very unsatisfying, unhappy experience." Surely, there were greener pastures elsewhere.

Less than a year before he vanished, Waterman was decidedly freaked out by the very prospect of disappearing on a mountain, saying of his first aborted Denali attempt: "If I didn't make it to the top, or if I died . . . nobody would know. It would be entirely a mystery. There is some kind of morbid pain involved with the fact that nobody will ever see you again."

Chip Brown, in his excellent biography of Guy Waterman, *Good Morning Midnight,* offers the following support for the theory that Johnny Waterman staged his disappearance (aside from the fact that his body was never located): An Alaska magistrate in consultation with the National Park Service waited six months after Waterman disappeared to hold a presumptive death hearing and issue a death certificate. The administrative procedure is typically scheduled within four to six weeks of when a climber is lost and presumed dead in the mountains of Denali National Park. The delay is both a tribute to Waterman's reputation for beating the odds and a testament to the fact that, even during his last days, he did not seem to be conspicuously out of touch with reality.

However, Brown and virtually everyone else who knew Waterman, including Johnny's father, Guy, accepted the idea of his demise. "In the end," Guy Waterman said, "the mountains were the only place Johnny could feel at home, so that's where he went to stay for good." In Guy Waterman's unpublished memoirs, he wrote of Johnny: "He was always at war with the world, never knew calm, always teetered on the verge of being out of control—and frequently was."

Guy Waterman chose April 1 as the anniversary of his son's death. Every year on that date, he would make a pilgrimage to the cairn he had erected around Johnny's hiking boots off the trail near the Franconia Ridge in the White Mountains of New Hampshire. The spot commands a stunning view, looking over Cannon Cliff and including the route that Johnny had pioneered when he was still a youngster—when times were better.

It wasn't surprising that Guy Waterman thought that in the end his boy had committed suicide. If that surmise is accurate, it marks another point of intersection between father and son. (Of suicidal impulses, Guy Waterman once wrote rhetorically of Johnny: "Where, after all, did [he] get them from?")

On February 6, 2000, Guy Waterman kissed his wife good-bye, told her to make bread, to be brave, and not to come out to porch to watch him walk off. He went into town, mailed letters to friends, hiked up Franconia Notch, sat down in the snow and wind, and let himself succumb to the cold.

Today, Guy Waterman's hiking boots sit next to his son Johnny's, inside a cairn in the White Mountains.

8 / INDEX

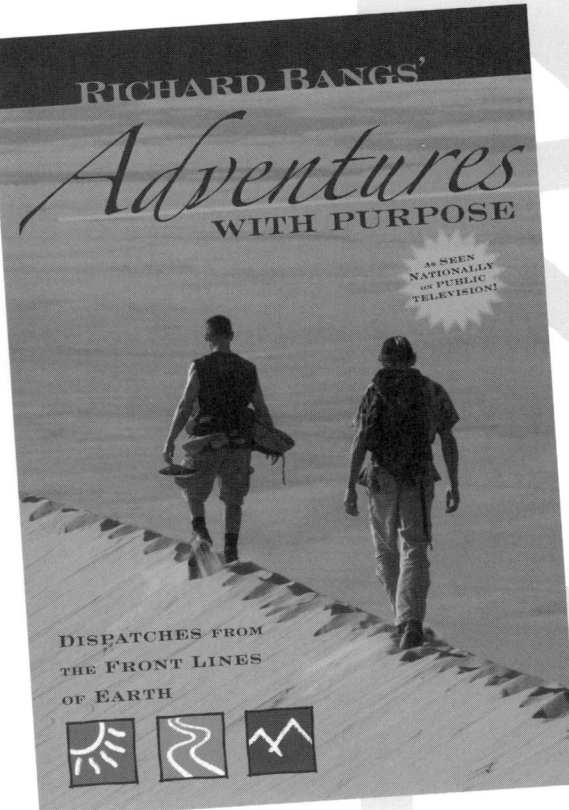

DEAR CUSTOMERS AND FRIENDS,

SUPPORTING YOUR INTEREST IN OUTDOOR ADVENTURE, travel, and an active lifestyle is central to our operations, from the authors we choose to the locations we detail to the way we design our books. Menasha Ridge Press was incorporated in 1982 by a group of veteran outdoorsmen and professional outfitters. For 25 years now, we've specialized in creating books that benefit the outdoors enthusiast.

Almost immediately, Menasha Ridge Press earned a reputation for revolutionizing outdoors- and travel-guidebook publishing. For such activities as canoeing, kayaking, hiking, backpacking, and mountain biking, we established new standards of quality that transformed the whole genre, resulting in outdoor-recreation guides of great sophistication and solid content. Menasha Ridge continues to be outdoor publishing's greatest innovator.

The folks at Menasha Ridge Press are as at home on a white-water river or mountain trail as they are editing a manuscript. The books we build for you are the best they can be, because we're responding to your needs. Plus, we use and depend on them ourselves.

We look forward to seeing you on the river or the trail. If you'd like to contact us directly, join in at **www.trekalong.com** or visit us at **www.menasharidge.com**. We thank you for your interest in our books and the natural world around us all.

SAFE TRAVELS,

Bob Sehlinger

BOB SEHLINGER
PUBLISHER